LET'S GET REAL™

Bringing
Authenticity and Wholeness
to Your Marriage

LET'S GET REAL™

DALE and JENA FOREHAND

NAVPRESS
Discipleship Inside Out™

NAVPRESS

Discipleship Inside Out™

NavPress is the publishing ministry of The Navigators, an international Christian organization and leader in personal spiritual development. NavPress is committed to helping people grow spiritually and enjoy lives of meaning and hope through personal and group resources that are biblically rooted, culturally relevant, and highly practical.

For a free catalog go to www.NavPress.com
or call 1.800.366.7788 in the United States or 1.800.839.4769 in Canada.

ISBN-13: 978-1-61521-689-5

Cover design by Arvid Wallen
Cover photo by Shutterstock/iofoto

Some of the anecdotal illustrations in this book are true to life and are included with the permission of the persons involved. All other illustrations are composites of real situations, and any resemblance to people living or dead is coincidental.

Unless otherwise identified, all Scripture quotations in this publication are taken from the *Holy Bible, New International Version*® (NIV®). Copyright © 1973, 1978, 1984 by International Bible Society. Used by permission of Zondervan. All rights reserved. Other versions used include: the New American Standard Bible® (NASB), Copyright © 1960, 1962, 1963, 1968, 1971, 1972, 1973, 1975, 1977, 1995 by The Lockman Foundation. Used by permission; All rights reserved; and the New King James Version (NKJV). Copyright © 1982 by Thomas Nelson, Inc. Used by permission. All rights reserved.

Printed in the United States of America

2 3 4 5 6 7 8 9 / 17 16 15 14 13 12

CONTENTS

LETTER FROM DALE AND JENA

Each of us has a story. Our stories involve different characters and circumstances but have one commonality: They all involve a journey. Journeys take us places. Yet each of us plays a part in choosing the journey's end.

The story that follows is our journey. It's the story of the death, burial, and resurrection of our marriage. But this story isn't about us. It's about the incredible truths we learn from God along the way that offer hope and abundant life when we walk in them. For as long as we have Jesus, we have hope.

Our marriage was saved purely by the grace of God. He revealed our selfish ways and helped us trust Him in obedience. God took us on a journey to wholeness. He helped us exchange religious activity for spiritual intimacy. We found that only when we as individuals pursued the heart of God and became whole in spirit, soul, and body could our marriage relationship become healthy and whole. It was here, and only here, that our marriage would bring glory to God. As a result, our house became a home where Jesus reigns as Lord.

Perhaps you have a good marriage but want it to be better. Perhaps your marriage is not what it should be. You may have a marriage that is struggling to survive. Maybe you're divorced, feeling devastated and alone. Whatever your circumstances, we encourage you to walk down a road less traveled.

We believe that fulfilling, lifelong marriages are the direct result of individuals who desire to grow in their personal relationship with Christ. There's a direct relationship between our intimacy with our heavenly Father and our intimacy with others.

This study won't be a tip and technique or quick fix for you. It's a study designed to look at the Word of God to learn how to have better relationships. Its impact will depend on you, your spouse, and your obedience to the Spirit's leading in your life. We know God's Word is true, that He is faithful, and He can do abundantly more than we could ever think or imagine if we will take Him at His Word and trust Him through His awesome power and grace.

To get the most from this study, prepare your hearts for your time with God as you read the pages that follow. Let us offer a few suggestions:

1. Ask the Holy Spirit to reveal to you areas in your life that need to be crucified. This study isn't for you to think about how much your spouse needs to change. Let this be a special time where God deals with you and you alone (see Psalm 139:23).

2. Ask the Lord to make your heart tender toward His truths and then give you the strength to walk in obedience to His truths. By His Spirit and your personal evaluation, much can be exposed to help you become as God wants you to be as you read each chapter (see John 8:32).

3. Ask the Comforter to join you in your journey. You'll need His strength and encouragement as you visit many places. As you are comforted, you'll be able to minister to others along the way. The fact is, we learn from one another and thus should share with one another what the Holy Spirit has revealed to us (see 2 Corinthians 1:3-4).

4. Ask God to make Him highly exalted in your life and draw you nearer to Him. If you want to get the most from this book, you

must be willing to let God go to the very depths of your soul and do His healing work (see James 4:8).

We are thrilled that God has divinely appointed this time for us. He always meets us where we are and takes us moment by moment to where He wants us to be. As you read our story, know that God has a story within your life and marriage. As He does His awesome work, molding and crafting you into His image, don't give up. Stay the course. Our relationships with other people and most importantly our relationship with Christ will never be the same as we yield ourselves to His leadership. Let the journey begin.

Chapter One

BROKEN PIECES

Now to Him who is able to do exceedingly abundantly above all that we ask or think . . .

Ephesians 3:20 (NKJV)

In 1996, our marriage had reached an all-time low. There was no love, no joy, and no relationship. Misplaced priorities and neglect had delivered us to the doorway of divorce. We'd brought two precious children into the world, Cole and Jorja. We'd built a nice house in a nice part of town. Dale and I were both extremely active in church. Dale was a new deacon in the church. I (Jena) was a leading soloist and had just finished writing our Easter musical. Together we taught a Sunday school class for young couples. From the outside looking in, we had the perfect marriage, the perfect life. In reality, both of us were doing life while neglecting our marriage.

After years of complacency, selfishness, and total disregard for each other, a marriage that had once borne beautiful fruit was withering. Our suppressed emotional pain had turned into a bitter cancer that turned love to hate and freedom to bondage. The wounds we inflicted on each other's hearts left us bleeding hopelessly. The pain was so intense we believed the only way to survive was to get out.

THE MARRIAGE SHATTERS

On a Saturday in July 1996, Dale walked into our home, took out my suitcases, and began to pack my clothes. He said the marriage was over and told me to get out of his house because he was finished with the relationship. I followed Dale into the bathroom as he packed my things. Dale closed the door behind me, held it shut, and began to hurl verbal attacks as Cole banged on the door to get in. When I attempted to leave, Dale held the door shut and laughed as I struggled to get out.

Dale grabbed our children, Cole (age five at the time) and Jorja (eighteen months), and loaded them into his car. Dale sped off to the golf course with the children because golf was a release for him. Later he left the children with his mother at the swimming pool. I drove to the pool, gathered the children, and headed to my sister's house while things settled. When Dale realized what I'd done, he was incredibly angry. I called Dale and explained that I was afraid of him and wanted to stay away until I felt safe again.

Internal frustrations and lack of control angered Dale. He became so enraged that he continued to verbally attack and threaten me. He demanded that I return the children. I became even more afraid for myself, Cole, and Jorja. After four days, I met Dale at a park so the children could play and visit with him. There was no conversation between the two of us. The tension was thick.

I didn't know Dale had gone to see a lawyer. The lawyer told Dale the kids were just as much his as they were mine and to just go and get them. For Dale, this sounded like a great plan.

The next week was Vacation Bible School at our church. I had responsibilities there so I brought the children and participated as if nothing had happened. While I was cleaning up at the end of the day, Cole was playing in the gym and Jorja was with me at the entrance. Dale drove up determined to take our children. I saw him and quickly ran into the gym to get Cole. As I sat Jorja on the ground and yelled for Cole to come to me, I turned around to see Dale grab Jorja and scramble to the car. Cole jumped into my arms and asked me what was happening and why Daddy was taking Jorja. Panicking, I repeatedly whispered in Cole's ear that it was all going to be okay. With Cole in my arms, I chased Dale to his car. He disappeared with our daughter while I watched in disbelief.

I returned to the gym where Dale's twin brother, Dave, yanked Cole out of my arms and knocked me to the ground as I fought to hang on to my child. As Dave ran with Cole to a car that waited outside, Cole screamed for me in hysteria. I sat on the gym floor, as Cole's voice echoed, "Mommy! Mommy! I want my mommy!" And then there was nothing—nothing but silence.

I sat in shock at what had just taken place. Though most everyone quickly disappeared, a few helped me to my feet and encouraged me to call the police. My family arrived to help while I was reporting the incident to a police officer. As he wrote the report, he explained that Dale was the father and there was nothing he could do about his taking the children. The best advice he could give was to call an attorney.

Meanwhile, Dale went to his parents' house, packed some bags, loaded the children into his car, and disappeared with them for seven days. They went to the U.S. Space and Rocket Center in Huntsville, Alabama. They traveled to Chattanooga, Tennessee, to peer through the big glass and see all the fish at the aquarium. For seven days, Dale ran from our problems while I lay in a small, dark bedroom in my sister's home, scared and alone.

After fruitless attempts to locate the children, I picked up the phone and called an attorney—something I'd never dreamed of doing. During my first visit, I was advised that the only way to get my children back into the state of Alabama was to file for a divorce. The attorney drew up the papers and an officer left to serve them to Dale.

On the back roads of a Tennessee highway, Dale's cell phone rang. It was his employer telling him they had just received papers that read, "Forehand versus Forehand." Dale's heart fell to the depths of his soul. We both realized we were about to face the most excruciating process we had ever experienced: divorce.

When I arrived at the courthouse, I was told it would be a long process unless Dale and I could negotiate with the aid of our lawyers. We both wanted full custody, however, and both refused to leave the marital residence. That left the judge with no choice but to place us back in the house together pending a divorce trial.

IN-HOUSE PRISON

For fifteen months we lived in one house, awaiting the trial date. Our home had now become a prison. Dale took the master bedroom and locked me out. I locked myself in Cole's bedroom, sleeping with him in his red wrought-iron bunk beds. Many nights I cried myself to sleep while our six-year-old son patted me sweetly on the back.

As time passed, we returned to court several times, each accusing the other of breaking the rules. The judge ruled that we must have the children in the residence by six every night because of our game playing and manipulation. Being bound to a curfew forced us to spend time together, causing our house to feel smaller with each passing day.

Because of Dale's anger and desire for control, he withheld all money from me. Being a stay-at-home mother, I was reduced to begging from Dale or borrowing from friends and family—a very humbling and shaming experience. Dale gave me a credit card but one false move and he'd rip it away.

We tried to conduct ourselves as if the other didn't exist. We locked doors, separated our clothes and food, and pulled our children from one parent to the other as we each tried to win their love. When we engaged in conversation, our talks escalated into full-fledged arguments that left us wounded and cold. Many fights became so heated that Cole would sit in the corner of the dining room and cry with his hands over his ears, begging for it to stop. We threw things, pointed our fingers, and verbally abused one another.

We tried to buy our children's love with gifts and keep the other from seeing them. Manipulation became a common behavior, and we showed no conscience in the process. The children quickly learned to manipulate too. There were many situations where they would work the circumstances to force us to be at odds with each other to get their way.

Christmas was a gut-wrenching experience. The lawyers made another trip to the judge because we couldn't agree on any terms. The children and I got one tree and placed it in the den, and then Dale took the children and purchased another tree for the dining room.

I had no money to buy gifts for the children, and Dale wouldn't give me any. So one afternoon, a friend picked me up and took me to Wal-Mart to purchase Christmas gifts for me to give them. I stood in the checkout line and cried at the reality of my life.

Christmas Eve finally came. I came out of the bedroom first and placed my Santa gifts out on the den floor. After I went back to my bedroom and locked my door, Dale came and displayed his part of Santa. The next morning was a smothering event as both of us put on our happy faces and pretended to be a family.

Things continued to unravel as two competing lawyers coached us in the ways of mischief. We paid private investigators and wore tape recorders to catch the other in some incriminating conversation. We tapped phones and kept perfect records to build our own cases. We provoked the other to anger so we could accuse each other of misconduct. Our house was a war zone, and the casualties were not only two adults but two beautiful children.

After living in this hell for fifteen months, my lawyer informed me our day in court was set. My lawyer was prepared, and there was a glimmer of hope that the end was in sight.

THE COURT DECREES

I entered a small courtroom with my lawyer at my side and a small box that represented my life. Dale did the same. The judge entered and took his place. The sound of the gavel meant only one thing: The lines were drawn and the final battle began.

The next four days we listened to family members and friends testify from the witness stand. They'd chosen sides, and their goal was to convince the judge what a terrible parent one of us was. Lies filled the courtroom. Our parents who once loved their child's spouse were now doing all they could to defend their own flesh and blood. With every comment came another penetrating stab of emotional pain. It felt as if our lives were being ripped to shreds. As the gavel fell for the last time, we left the courthouse with our arms full of broken pieces.

We were told to go back to our house together pending the results of the trial. Four weeks of waiting were smothering as we waited for the outcome. We finally received the papers. The divorce was final, and joint custody was awarded.

Hallelujah, it was finally over—or was it? My (Jena) depression and anger only increased. I rode an emotional roller coaster as I went from the elation of finality to the frustration of always having to communicate with Dale about matters regarding the children. The marriage was over, but life continued. The struggles for personal agendas, strategic plans, and individual time with the children escalated. We argued about everything pertaining to our children before we could make a decision. Every other weekend, as we passed the children to the other, we felt as if our hearts were physically being ripped apart. The anger, frustration, and pain were indescribable.

Divorce is a forever funeral as part of you dies every other weekend while your child grips your neck and begs you not to leave. Divorce is what I thought I wanted, yet I was more miserable than I had ever been. Divorce affects you physically, emotionally, and spiritually. All that's left is a shattered reflection of what used to be. And the pain associated with it cannot be compared to anything except a grievous death.

GETTING REAL

Fortunately, our story didn't end there. God didn't look down from the glory of heaven and say, "Dale and Jena, you have messed things up so badly that I can't fix it anymore." Instead, He graciously said, "I'll wipe this clean and help you start over if you will let Me." Two very broken people, not knowing what the other was doing, dragged themselves to the foot of the cross and fell at their Savior's feet, begging for His forgiveness and help.

One Wednesday morning, four weeks after the final verdict, I called Dale to discuss some gymnastics arrangements for Jorja. Dale, still wounded from the previous battle, told me that he would not be taking Jorja anywhere when she was with him, and another argument began. Our yelling was so intense that Dale had to close his office door to muffle the sound.

I (Jena) chose to reveal myself that day so Dale could briefly peek into my heart. It was the scariest thing I'd ever done, but God was pushing me to obey His prompting. These words came from my heart in the middle of this downward-spiraling conversation: "Dale, what have we done? Why don't you just come get me and let's fix this thing." Like a bolt of lightning, Dale heard words that shocked him to the bone.

Dale was faced with a choice. Would he respond with fear, pride, or anger, or would he return my tenderness of heart with truth of his own? Dale responded with this simple statement: "I can't look at the feet of our children without seeing you." That statement was like a bouquet of roses to me. I didn't think he cared about what I looked like, much less my feet. The Spirit of the Lord began at that very moment to melt the hardened mess of our hearts. The pride, anger, bitterness, resentment, and sheer hatred began to peel back one layer at a time. Within minutes Dale and I were pouring out our hearts while sobbing uncontrollably.

Dale drove to the house where I was staying. He knocked on the door, and a friend of mine who had testified against him in court answered. With great shock and fear on her face, she called for me to come outside. Dale spoke these words from his heart: "Jena, I don't know what all of this means, but I know it's the right thing to do." He kissed me on the cheek and drove away.

We spent the next four months in frequent marriage counseling with a godly Christian counselor who walked us through the healing process. There were hard days when it seemed like we tap-danced on the painful places where we had sworn never to return. Some days seemed like all was fresh and new while others made us question our decision to return to each other. At the end of four months, there was no question in either of our minds. Remarriage was what God wanted. So on December 21, 1997, we were remarried to the glory of God.

On the morning of our remarriage, Cole entered our bedroom and said, "Since you two are getting together with each other, I think I would like to get together with God." At the foot of our bed, our son prayed with us to receive Jesus as His Savior. Ephesians 3:20 says, "Now to Him who is able to do exceedingly abundantly above all that we ask or think . . ." (NKJV). God not only brought our marriage back together but redeemed our precious child into His family. His plans are truly greater than we could ever imagine.

Chapter 2

SAFE MATES

"Therefore everyone who hears these words of mine and puts them into practice is like a wise man who built his house on the rock. The rain came down, the streams rose, and the winds blew and beat against that house; yet it did not fall, because it had its foundation on the rock. But everyone who hears these words of mine and does not put them into practice is like a foolish man who built his house on sand. The rain came down, the streams rose, and the winds blew and beat against that house, and it fell with a great crash." When Jesus had finished saying these things, the crowds were amazed at his teaching.

Matthew 7:24-28

If you read our story, you will recognize how broken our marriage was and how awesome our God is! How do the couples you know react when the streams of stress hit their house? Are they handling it like we did, just walking away and allowing their home to come crashing down? Or are they willing to do whatever it takes to strengthen their home to protect it against the inevitable storms?

....

We're convinced of this: We can hear
about the right things to do, but until we put
them into practice, they're useless.

....

We're convinced of this: We can hear about the right things to do, but until we put them into practice, they're useless. We discovered the hard way that God's ways and God's Word really are the keys to having a successful marriage. But it's so much more than just knowing what God's ways are and knowing what His Word says. It's in applying His Word and His ways to our daily lives that change really takes place. We only become proficient with practice. Your marriage is no exception.

Applying God's Word and ways in our lives has had an eternal impact on us, our marriage, our family, and our friendships. We're excited to share with you some of the amazing, transforming truths we've learned in this process of building a house that can stand the test of time. It's our prayer that as you study and practice what you learn, you too will begin the process of allowing God to transform your marriage into a happy, fulfilling, and strong house that will withstand the storms of life.

1. Take a moment to ask the Holy Spirit, your Helper, to enlighten you to truth. Then reread Matthew 7:24-28, the Scripture at the beginning of this chapter.

Based on this Scripture, what might be some of the rains and winds that are currently beating on the house of your marriage?

Often we hear answers such as financial struggles, lack of intimacy, lack of communication, he or she doesn't understand me, or he or she is too stubborn. We ask this question for two reasons: one, so you know you're not alone—that other marriages are just like yours, and two, so after you've applied God's ways and Word to your marriage, you'll be able to look back and see what God can do when we get real with Him and with each other.

The rock in Jesus' example is the applied Word of God. No marriage resource will be of any value unless the principles taught are practiced within your marriage. We're going to ask you to apply God's Word to your marriage. We know God will strengthen your marriage and enable you to withstand all the rains and winds that come against it, helping you develop a fulfilling marriage that lasts forever. Will you commit to practice the truths you learn through this study?

Ask God even now to help you hear His truth and then put it into practice.

SAFE MATES

Once God restored our marriage, we realized there was still much work ahead of us. First, we looked back to discover how we got to such a broken place. What we uncovered was the slow erosion of connectedness in our first marriage. Over time, we became disconnected through busyness, neglect, and the demands of life that overshadowed our relationship.

We just didn't feel safe with one another. When we talk about safety or becoming *safe mates*, we're talking about an emotional safety where a husband and wife can freely, without fear, open their hearts to one another. We realized we had lost all emotional safety in our marriage and fear of the other's response had kept us emotionally severed. Fear in marriage is a huge barrier to being connected. Many couples are afraid to expose their hearts or share with their spouses. Many are emotionally hidden behind huge walls of self-protection. They have decided that it's safer to keep their hearts close and closed. When safety is lost, couples find themselves in stagnant, nonemotional relationships. They usually default to each one playing their roles well while pouring their lives into their kids, careers, and civic or church service.

2. Does this sound like you? If so, how have you seen this occur in your marriage? If not, what about your marriage is different?

3. According to 2 Timothy 1:7, what has God offered us in place of fear?

4. What does a spirit of power, love, and self-discipline look like in a safe marriage?

5. Based on Proverbs 18:10, where is our ultimate safety found?

God used these two scriptural truths to help us regain the safety we'd lost. In the midst of great uncertainty and fear, we found the power to open up to one another once again through Christ. We relied on the truth that regardless of what happened, regardless of one another's response, our ultimate safety was found first and foremost in the person of Jesus Christ. He is faithful, good, loving, with us, our friend, and so much more. We are safe with Him. Real, authentic connectedness in marriage develops when we display the safe character of Christ.

....

Real, authentic connectedness in marriage
develops when we display the safe
character of Christ.

....

Armed with these promises, you too can press through your fears, leaning on His strength to open or reopen your heart so that you can begin to find emotional safety once again in your relationship.

This week, we'll be looking at the five elements of becoming a safe mate, based on the person of Jesus Christ, our strong tower of safety. His life will be our guide to getting real by reconnecting with our spouse and developing emotional safety in our marriages. As each element is revealed, evaluate how safe you are as a spouse and then ask the Lord to help you take some small steps in practicing these safety truths in your marriage.

BEING AVAILABLE

One of the names of Christ is "Emmanuel—God with us." He is always available. You don't have to take a number, get in line, or wait your turn. Just as Christ is available to us, we must also be available for one another! Unfortunately, many couples today are simply too busy to be available. Their marriage is full of separate schedules, tasks to be done, places to go, and lists to check off. It happened to us. The only time we talked was when there was a problem to fix or a schedule to arrange. Dale was busy with work and Jena was busy caring for kids and serving at church. In the process we lost our connectedness. There were many times when we were in the same room but miles apart emotionally. There's a big difference between being in close proximity and being close in heart!

> There's a big difference between being in
> close proximity and being close in heart!

I remember one evening when I (Dale) was watching a baseball game. Jena wanted to talk with me, but I was way too preoccupied with the game to listen. Now, Jena used to have some really stinky feet, so to get my attention, she quietly took off her shoes and placed one under my nose. Whew, did that get my attention! While it wouldn't be the method we'd recommend, I recognized that without saying a word I was communicating to Jena that the baseball game was more important than her. Since then, I make it a point to turn off the television and give Jena my full attention when she needs to talk to me. That's what I want her to do for me, and it communicates that she is more valuable to me than anything else this world could offer. Likewise, Jena graciously asks if she can talk or needs to wait until the game is over. Marriage is a partnership, and it takes both people growing and learning how to do life together.

Webster defines being *available* as "present or ready for immediate use; willing to do something."[1] My (Jena's) mother always told me to have the house and kids clean with food on the table so that Dale could come home to a peaceful place after a long day at work. However, sometimes the chaos of life and the unexpected accidents that occurred made our home anything but peaceful. Dale would come in the door and I'd be so preoccupied with dinner and schoolwork that I didn't even welcome him home or ask about his day. Although I was doing all those activities for him, I was missing his heart in the process. Thank God for second and third chances. Now I try to make it a point to welcome him home with loving arms, even if everything isn't perfect at the time.

6. Think of a time when your spouse was available for you. How did it make you feel?

In marriage we may be present but not always ready to receive and serve one another. Being available is more than just being bodily present. It's being ready and willing to do whatever is needed whether it's listening, advising, encouraging, or understanding. It means you're willing to die to your own selfish desires and embrace one another's hearts. You see this in Christ.

In Revelation 3:20, Jesus is standing at the door and knocking. He promises to come in if anyone opens the door. Many believe that this Scripture was written for those who need to be saved. However, Revelation 3:20 was written to Christians—those who are already saved! Jesus desires intimacy, community, fellowship, and relationship with us. He desires more for you than just eternal security from hell. Salvation is the beginning of a journey toward a close relationship with Christ—not the end. Like Jesus, we too desire more than just getting married and that being the end. We want a close connectedness in our relationship.

Jesus is always available to us. He stands at the door of our hearts ready to join us in intimate relationship. To display His character in our marriages, we must do the same. Today, you can begin to make yourself available in your marriage by practicing the very character of our Savior.

Being Approachable

7. Take a moment to write a prayer to the Lord, asking Him to guide you and teach you.

8. Think of the person who is most intimidating for you to talk to. What makes them that way? Is it their demeanor, body language, or attitude? Perhaps you've had problems dealing with them or they've snapped at you during previous conversations. Whatever the circumstances, being a safe mate requires learning how to be approachable.

List some characteristics of an approachable person.

Many times in our marriage, we just didn't feel the freedom to approach each other. It's like there's an invisible wall. You know something is just not right between you, but you dare not approach it. You choose to walk around with this hidden tension and unsettled fear. For us, it began with cold shoulders, short answers, and quick comebacks. It escalated to complete rejection, both physically and emotionally, as well as manipulation through the silent treatment, pouting, criticism, and condemnation. When you're continually hurt in your marriage, you condition yourself by becoming closed, protected, and unapproachable. All of these self-protecting, manipulative, relational responses destroy safety in marriage. Unhealthy couples who feel unsafe, insecure, and insignificant try to fix these feelings through sex. For a few days they feel better about their relationship. This only masks the real problems, and sooner or later, the issues return. More dejected and confused than before, couples find themselves back in the same emotionally unsafe place, feeling stuck.

I (Jena) can remember the fear I felt as I began to put this principle into practice. Since our first marriage had been so hurtful, I was very closed. As I realized this was a new and scary place for Dale too, I began by faith to take small steps to allow Dale back into my life, even sharing that I was a bit afraid. Dale was very gracious and confessed that he was scared too. We slowly began to open our hearts to each other.

Consider for a moment the Old Testament duties of the high priest. The Old Covenant required the high priest to crawl under the veil and offer sacrifices for the atonement of the people's sins. Only the high priest was allowed in the Holy of Holies, the most sacred place before God. As the high priest entered under the veil, a rope was tied to his ankle in case he was struck dead because of his own uncleanness or failure to complete his duties properly. Temple servants could drag him out by the rope and send another priest in his stead. Does that sound like an approachable and safe place to you?

9. Read Hebrews 4:16, and describe what happened when Jesus died for us.

Jesus Christ came, fully available, and gave Himself as our High Priest. He offered Himself as the once-and-for-all sacrifice for our sins, and the veil of the temple was torn from top to bottom. God's Word says that because of Jesus' sacrifice, all of us can boldly approach His throne to receive mercy and find grace to help us in our every time of need. Ephesians 3:12 says, "In him and through faith in him we may approach God with freedom and confidence." Now, that sounds like safety! We are totally welcome to approach God through Jesus at any time, any place, with any thing. Following Jesus' example of being fully approachable, we too can begin to practice this in our marriages.

What's the best way to welcome children? We bend down and stretch out our arms to welcome them with a big hug. They run into our open arms, almost knocking us over with delight, while we hold them tightly and lovingly.

10. In Mark 9:36-37, how was Jesus described as He interacted with the child?

How would you feel if you saw Jesus holding out His outstretched arms to you? He did just that more than 2,000 years ago on a tree at Calvary. His arms are still open today to anyone who will run to Him. He is fully approachable, and we can be too.

When I (Jena) was growing up, there was this man in my church who always had Dum-dum suckers for the children. His name was Pops! He knew my favorite flavor was cream soda. Every Sunday I would go looking for Pops because he was warm and welcoming. I knew I could fully approach him. It really wasn't about the candy he gave me, it was about how loved I felt in his presence. The fact that he remembered my favorite flavor made me feel so special and loved. Jesus showed us this when He interacted with children. Children don't run to people who aren't safe. They look for love and acceptance. Within our marriage relationship, we want to feel as warm, welcomed, and loved in our spouse's presence as I did with Pops—fully loved and accepted.

....

Being a *safe mate* means you
welcome your spouse with open arms.

....

Being a *safe mate* means you welcome your spouse with open arms. It means they aren't fearful about coming to you and revealing their heart. Is this true of your relationship? Can you approach one another with anything? If you haven't been approachable in the past, maybe it's time to confess and seek forgiveness. Will you let Christ approach you, and will you approach Christ? Will you be willing to approach your spouse and make yourself more approachable in return?

As you begin to practice approaching God and your spouse, as well as becoming more approachable, a new depth of connectedness will grow in your relationships. Welcome God and your spouse into conversation and fellowship with outstretched arms.

BEING ACCEPTABLE

As we grow in safety, we need to practice being more than available and approachable. We must also learn to be accepting of our spouses. There are times when we haven't been accepting of what our husband or wife shares with us. At times, it feels like our spouse only tells us what we're doing wrong

> Approach the Lord with confidence today: Lord, I come to You and ask that You help me understand Your truth. In Jesus' name, Amen.

and how we've hurt them. Our first response is to be defensive. We feel they should control their emotions, stop being so sensitive, and just get over it. Ever said those words? Ever heard those words? Remarks like these can be definite safety-busters.

These responses all show a lack of acceptance: sarcasm, rebuttal, interruption, and rejection. Alternatively, these responses show acceptance: listening, receiving what your spouse has to say, and responding to what you have heard. Attitude in all of these responses is also critical.

11. When it comes to dealing with others, how does Ephesians 4:2 command us to be?

Boy, did we mess this up during the early years of our marriage! Many days, we were guilty of partially listening and fully responding. Our defenses were up so high we couldn't even receive or properly evaluate what was shared. We quickly jumped to defense mode, especially when we felt we were being blamed. We never heard the rest of what was said and quickly made a mental list of everything that would give us leverage in winning the battle.

Your spouse is not your enemy.

Two of the greatest truths we learned to hold onto in our marriage are these: First of all, your spouse is not your enemy. There is no need to be defensive—especially without first completely hearing what your spouse is trying to say. Second, you must trust that the heart of your spouse desires good for you.

We've worked hard at remembering both of these truths. In the midst of our conflicts, misunderstandings, or days where we were simply selfish and it was all about us, we reminded each other: We're not enemies and our hearts toward each other are good. A *safe mate* accepts what their spouse shares and encourages them to speak freely without fear of the other's response.

12. Why might we sometimes struggle with accepting our spouses?

The power of acceptance in marriage is a wonderful thing. It's rarely experienced, however. Many times, the very thing that drew us to one another becomes a huge irritation, and we no longer accept our spouses just as they are. For example, one thing that endeared Jena to me (Dale) was her outgoing, bubbly, people-loving personality. During the early years of our marriage, we often got together with friends, playing cards and games, and going to sporting events. I loved this about her when we were dating but hated it after we were married. That walking, talking, bundle of fun was spending more of her time and attention with our friends than with me! Being a super-sensitive twenty-four-year-old, seeking to get some attention, I would make Jena the butt of my jokes, hoping to stunt her joy and regain some of her attention. I no longer accepted Jena for who she was. Jena tried to tell me how hurt she felt. "Tonight when you made me the butt of your jokes, it really hurt my feelings." Again, being the super-sensitive twenty-four-year-old, I responded, "Give me a break! It was just a joke! Get over it!" I didn't want to accept what Jena had to share and she no longer saw me as available, approachable, or very accepting of her. Allowing this to go on in various forms builds walls around hearts and destroys emotional safety.

We've had to work hard at not interrupting, jumping to conclusions, and becoming defensive. Listening to what Jena says and then responding in a loving way, even if it means admitting what I did was wrong is tough! What I should have said was, "You know, Babe, I didn't mean to embarrass you. I just wanted some of your attention and thought I could do it by being funny. It was wrong for me to do it at your expense. I'm sorry. Will you forgive me?" Accepting what your spouse shares and owning the responsibility for your hurtful actions or words promotes growth and healing. Accepting your spouse for who

God made him or her to be, even if it's different from you, offers freedom in your marriage. This strengthens your relationship and develops a connectedness that God uses to draw you closer to one another.

Another common attack on the power of acceptance in a marriage is the desire to change one another. Many couples spend a lot of energy trying to control and change each other. Because we often marry our opposites, we find ourselves battling viewpoints, approaches, and resolutions. I (Jena) remember counseling a friend of ours with Dale. As we listened, she described how her husband didn't think or act like she did, like the same things she did, or parent like she did. On and on the list went until she finally said, "If he would just act, think, and look like me, our marriage would be just fine." Dale asked her this question: "Is it more important to you that your husband look like you or that he look like Jesus?" As I heard Dale say this, it dawned on me that I'd been guilty of the same mistake. The Holy Spirit brought to mind many times when I had tried to tweak Dale into my image instead of praying that God would transform him into His image. The power of acceptance is when we accept our spouses where they are, but we love them enough not to leave them there.

....

The power of acceptance is when we accept our spouses where they are, but we love them enough not to leave them there.

....

Today I've turned my tweaking into praying. God doesn't need my help to mold Dale into His image. I have the privilege of praying for him and then staying out of the way as God does His work. I've also learned to practice verbally expressing the differences between Dale and me and appreciating them. After all, God may have brought Dale into my life just to reveal some areas in my life that need some tweaking of their own.

Again, Jesus is the perfect example to follow. God knew we would need His Word, as well as someone in bodily form to show us how to put His character into practice.

13. Read John 1:14. What two things did Jesus demonstrate on earth?

If Jesus only presented truth, it would show us we could never measure up. If Jesus only offered grace, we'd be tempted to live however we wanted because He'd always forgive. Jesus came with both grace and truth. He presented the truth and then offered the grace to help us grow as we strive to be like Him. The life of Christ is a clear example of being available and approachable. He accepted others with great love. He let people know they didn't have to have it all together and be perfect to be in relationship with Him. He loved people exactly the way they were, then gracefully and lovingly led them to change. If you're going to live as a *safe mate*, then display the power of acceptance in your marriage by following Christ's example. Accept your spouse where they are, then lovingly encourage them to grow into Christlikeness.

BEING ACCOUNTABLE

14. Write your own prayer as you begin this section of study.

Being a *safe mate* isn't easy. A great marriage only comes with great work. Sometimes it feels like it would be easier to let things go and play your role well. Yet none of us really want the resulting disconnectedness in our marriages. We must press on to display the character of Christ.

....

A great marriage only comes with great work.

....

15. In the following Scriptures, circle what God will do and put a square around what you must do:

Let us not become weary in doing good, for at the proper time we will reap a harvest if we do not give up. (Galatians 6:9)

He gives strength to the weary and increases the power of the weak. (Isaiah 40:29)

Let these be an encouragement to your soul. Stay the course. Your marriage matters. If you cooperate with God, He'll bring authenticity and wholeness to your marriage.

Now it's time to look at accountability in marriage. Let's be real, accountability in marriage is difficult. It certainly can be mishandled. Sometimes couples use it as a platform to judge each other's lives. Author John Eldredge once stated that accountability has been reduced to being one another's parole officer.[2] Instead of parole officers in our marriages, we need partners.

Other couples use accountability to cause their spouse to hide behind a façade. They fear the disappointment and rejection of being fully known. So they hide their concerns, true selves, and past baggage. Connectedness is strained because accountability is limited to the extent that you allow others into your life. Our fears of rejection, accusation, and condemnation (just to name a few) can be very motivating. Add the dependency on the approval of others, and there's a big motivation to keep our true selves hidden. Our hearts are so full of pride that we hesitate to admit our faults and needs. Excuses and justifications are easier than looking within. If a marriage consists of judgment and condemnation, fear and performance, or pride and justification, then the safety in marriage is eroding. This breeds resistance and resentment in the relationship.

> ## Accountability is limited to the extent that you allow others into your life.

Here's great news: When truly God-honoring accountability takes place, the rewards are significant. The greatest reward is that you no longer have to travel your journey to Christlikeness alone. God didn't create you to go through life alone. You were made in the image of a relational God who created you as a relational person (see Genesis 1:27). This is why becoming *safe mates* and the pursuit of genuine connectedness is critical for your marriage. Without it, we will all remain the same and never attain the goal of being like Christ.

A healthy level of accountability in your marriage relies on living out the first three principles (being available, approachable, and acceptable). It's hard to make withdrawals from one another without first making deposits. We all know what happens without deposits—bankruptcy.

> ## It's hard to make withdrawals from one another without first making deposits.

Here's an example. Jena went to the doctor due to vocal problems. The doctor told her to drink lots of water and avoid her favorite drink, Dr Pepper. She came home and shared with me (Dale) the doctor's advice while I was watching a baseball game. Instead of receiving her as a *safe mate*, I minimized her feelings, saying the whole thing was silly, and scolded her for interrupting the game. Realizing that I screwed up, I decided to fix this by taking her to dinner. We didn't speak all the way to the restaurant. Our waitress arrived to take our drink order and Jena replied, "I'll have the biggest honkin' Dr Pepper you've got." I piped up with, "Oh no, she interrupted my baseball game for this. She'll have water."

I didn't demonstrate the first principles of being safe with Jena, so I have no business holding her accountable. You can bet Jena will be resentful of me telling her what to do and resistant to my help in the future. Accountability without safety will result in resentment and resistance. But if I've been available to listen to her, approachable by turning to her and receiving her, and accepting of what she has to say about the doctor, then I can respond to her at the restaurant, "Hey, babe, don't you think you should drink water? The Doctor said it would be better for you," and she would respond much differently. This is holding her heart well. This is how to avoid damaged feelings, promote growth, and strengthen your relationship.

> ### Accountability without safety will result in resentment and resistance.

To create an environment for healthy accountability, pursue these four elements: honesty, humility, ownership, and partnership. Each of these plays a vital part in creating the environment where you can mutually grow.

16. Look at John 8:32 and write down what honesty brings.

Without honesty, it will be hard to know where and how to help one another.

17. Based on Matthew 7:3, what might you try to do without humility?

Without humility, spouses can easily focus on the speck in their partner's eye while disregarding the beam in their own.

18. According to Galatians 6:5, what are we supposed to carry?

Without ownership, a spouse will tend to become the victim and not carry his/her own load.

19. What does Ecclesiastes 4:9-12 tell us?

Without partnership, you'll become isolated and isolation thwarts intimacy.

20. Read Proverbs 27:17. Notice it uses the word *sharpen* and not *grate*. Think about the differences between sharpening and grating (the purpose, the process, the result). How can you sharpen your spouse instead of grate him or her?

21. What specific guideline does God show us for accountability in 1 Corinthians 4:21?

In a safe marriage, gentle accountability yields righteousness and healing (see Hebrews 12:11-13). Remember Jesus' perfect example of healthy accountability in John 1:14. He came with both grace and truth. Jesus holds us accountable by His Word while giving us grace as we try to live up to it. He speaks the hard truths to us and then gives us His Spirit to help us live it out. May your marriage be found full of grace and truth.

BEING VULNERABLE

> Holy Spirit, give me ears to hear what You have to say to me right now. I want to be a safe mate. I want to have a connectedness with my spouse the way You designed it to be—the same way You want to be connected to me. Help me find ways to demonstrate safety to my spouse and give me the grace to do it. In Jesus' name I ask, Amen.

We began our study with the principles of safety because we realize that unless a couple can move back toward each other and reconnect, they'll have a difficult time growing together through the study. Developing safety in your marriage can start now by taking small steps toward connecting or reconnecting with each other.

22. Refresh your memory by writing down the first four principles of being a *safe mate*.

It's only after the first four elements of safety have been established that the last quality will be exemplified without any hidden agendas or personal reservations.

Vulnerability is the final principle of safety. To us, true vulnerability means deeply revealing yourself, legitimately desiring but never demanding a loving response. It's the "no strings attached" principle of being a *safe mate.* Unfortunately, there's a lot of manipulation and hidden agendas in marriage. There are strings attached to many of our choices, behaviors, and conversations.

In the early years of our marriage, I (Dale) would do things to get my way. I might work around the house because I wanted to go play golf. Or I might say certain things or buy certain gifts because I wanted sex, because sex (physical connectedness) is often the way guys get emotionally connected to their wives. Women, on the other hand, desire emotional connection that leads to the physical. Dr. Kevin Leman got it right when he said that "sex erases problems for men, but problems erase sex for women."[3] No wonder true vulnerability is so hard in marriage! We want the same thing—intimacy and connectedness. We just go about it in opposite ways. In our marriage, we've learned that sometimes Dale needs to have sex so he can talk intimately, and sometimes Jena needs to talk intimately so she can be comfortable having sex. It's a give and take, and the safer you are with one another the smoother this becomes.

As good and vital as sex is to a marriage, sex is not intimacy and vulnerability. If sex was intimacy, then the United States of America would be one of the most intimate nations in the world! Intimacy is simply, "into me, I will let you see." Sex can't replace intimacy, but it can be a road to it for men and a response to it for women. True vulnerability is the opening up of your heart to another, revealing your hopes, your dreams, your feelings, your passions, your failures, and your struggles to one another.

23. In John 15:15, what describes the vulnerability of Jesus to His disciples?

Jesus was the epitome of being vulnerable. He deeply revealed Himself, legitimately desiring, but never demanding, a loving response. Everything the Father told Jesus, He disclosed to the disciples. They saw into Him completely.

Many of you are thinking all this sounds scary, mushy, gushy, warm, and fuzzy. But before you write it off as undesirable and impossible, hear us out. We had an aha moment during our last counseling session before we remarried. Our counselor asked us to sit knee to knee and confess how we had contributed to the breakdown of our marriage relationship. What happened birthed this teaching on vulnerability.

Jena began to cry. She dropped her head and couldn't look at me (Dale). Our counselor got out of her seat, knelt beside Jena's chair, and gently lifted her head. It reminds us that God is the lifter of our heads (see Psalm 3:3). She tenderly asked, "Jena, what are you afraid of?" Jena replied, "Over the course of our marriage, I have repeatedly taken my heart out and placed it in Dale's hands only to have him squeeze the life out of it. I am afraid to place my heart back in his hands again because I don't think I can survive another squeeze!" As I heard these words, it hit me in the core of my being. For the first time I realized I was not a *safe mate* to Jena. Crying, I got on my knees and replied, "Jena, if you will give me one more chance, I commit to try—with God's help—to never squeeze your heart again." This openness, vulnerability, and authentic intimacy broke down the walls we'd built around our hearts. We both committed that day to give each other another chance and go hard after the principles of safety.

We wish we could tell you that we've never messed up. We're imperfect people and there is no perfect marriage. However, we worship a perfect Savior who daily provides His grace, mercy, strength, and love to help us. On the days we don't do so well, we're thankful for the forgiveness we receive and are commanded to give. We are living examples that even though emotional safety might be lost in a marriage, it can be restored by becoming a *safe mate*. God will honor your efforts and obedience just as He did ours.

The five principles of safety, based on the character of Jesus Christ, build an upward spiral. As you make yourself available and approachable, you begin to receive healthy communication from your spouse. As you positively accept one another, you give and receive accountability. Vulnerability becomes more natural. As openness develops, you're empowered to become more available and approachable. And the upward spiral of growth continues.

If there's a lack of emotional safety in your marriage, there's hope for you. Perhaps you need to acknowledge where you haven't been a *safe mate* and haven't held your spouse's heart well. Perhaps you need a fresh start or a second chance. Why not ask for forgiveness and let today be the first day of rebuilding safety in your relationship? Authentic safety and intimacy is attainable if you take even small steps in applying God's Word in your marriage. Small changes can make large differences in your marriage.

The life of Christ showed us safety in its purest and perfect form. He was safe then and is still safe today. He is always available. He's always approachable. He's wholly accepting of us. He holds us accountable by His Word and the convicting power of the Holy Spirit. And He was vulnerable all the way to the cross.

This week's study is the foundation on which we'll build. The depth of growth for you individually and in your relationship with your spouse is contingent on the safety found in an intimate relationship with Christ. Out of the overflow of that relationship, God by His divine wisdom and power, will enable you to become a *safe mate*. If you've never accepted Christ as your Lord and Savior, go to the appendix at the end of this study and find out how you can experience safety and intimacy with Jesus.

Our prayer is that through the remaining weeks you'll accept the challenge to practice safety. Christ is the safest person there is. So run to Him and then take that safety into your marriage. You will experience a deeper walk with God, and your relationship with your spouse will thrive. Both can become a beautiful testimony of the goodness and grace of our Lord.

TAKING ACTION

Occasionally we'll ask you to do some honest self-evaluation. Do *not* evaluate your spouse. Let them do that with the Lord. I (Jena) have found that if I'm busy digging weeds out of Dale's yard, my own yard goes unattended and develops a bunch of weeds. Don't beat yourself up either. Just identify areas for improvement.

24. Prayerfully rate yourself on each of these elements, with "1" being an element that needs improvement and "5" being an element you demonstrate consistently.

Am I available?	1	2	3	4	5
Am I approachable?	1	2	3	4	5
Am I accepting?	1	2	3	4	5
Am I accountable?	1	2	3	4	5
Am I vulnerable?	1	2	3	4	5

25. Where did you rate the highest?

26. How can you capitalize on this area of strength?

27. Which element of safety do you most want to work on?

28. What one step can you take to begin improving safety in this element?

Try to share your findings with your spouse and commit to work toward better safety together. Affirm your spouse regarding his or her strengths. Commit to pray for each other and for your marriage as you both venture into weaker areas of safety in your relationship. Remember to stay in your own yard unless asked.

Higher-Risk Option: Based on where you are relationally, you may want to ask your spouse where they think you're doing well and where you need some work. This can promote great conversation and growth for both of you. If you do decide to ask these questions, be sure you're genuinely open to hearing the answer and ready to implement change. Don't ask if you're not ready to hear the truth.

Bringing authenticity and wholeness to your marriage matters. It matters to God, to your future, and to the generations that follow. The strength of our marriages determines the strength of our churches, communities, workplaces, and ministries. So be deliberate, be creative, and watch what God does as He helps you create an environment of safety in your marriage.

SAFE MATES

John 4—The Woman at the Well

Jesus _____ and _____ the
principles of safety in relationships (John 3:16, "whosoever").

Our challenge is to do the same (Matthew 7:24-27).

Safe Mates Principle #1: Be _____
(John 4:4-6).

Jesus _____ and _____
_____ (Luke 9:23; Philippians 2:3-4).

Safe Mates Principle #2: Be _____
(John 4:6-8; Proverbs 15:30; Matthew 11:28).

_____ has the power to risk or walk away.

_____ has the power to be closed
or open.

Safe Mates Principle #3: Be _____

(John 4:9-15; Romans 15:7).

Jesus showed us how when He _____

(empathy: to walk in one another's moccasins), _____

_____ , and was _____ .

Safe Mates Principle #4: Be _____

(John 4:16-24).

Biblically, this means that we _____

_____ .

When we do this, it _____

_____ (Ephesians 4:15; 1 Corinthians 4:21; Galatians 6:1).

Safe Mates Principle #5: Be _____

(John 4:25-39).

Vulnerability is deeply revealing yourself, legitimately desiring, but never demanding, a loving response.

When we are vulnerable, we avail ourselves to be _____

_____ and _____ .

These five elements are progressive. Don't miss a step or you'll breed resistance and resentment.

Building on the characteristics of Jesus to become a safe mate creates an environment of freedom for you and your spouse to transform into His likeness (Ephesians 2:22).

Now turn to appendix A (page 177) and record your resolution.

Chapter Three

EMPTY HEARTS, EMPTY HOMES

The God of our Lord Jesus Christ, the glorious Father, may give you the Spirit of wisdom and revelation, so that you may know him better.

Ephesians 1:17

In the movie *Fireproof*, John tells his son Caleb something profound: "You can't love her . . . because you can't give her what you don't have." What an amazingly true statement. Many people are wrapped up in their individual neediness. When this is combined with wrong motives and voids in their lives, marriage can be really empty. In other words, empty hearts lead to empty homes. Through our journey toward authenticity and wholeness we've found some specific and tangible root needs in marriage, and we're very excited to share what we've learned.

We met a couple who'd been married only two weeks. They were goo-gooing at each other continually. Pumpkin was their pet name for each other. They felt they had the perfect marriage. They had big aspirations and life was grand.

Now meet Adam and Eve. Their new marriage was the utopian honeymoon in the Garden of Eden. They had the perfect marriage in the perfect place. Adam was the king and Eve was his queen. They were complete and content. We call this flawless scenario "marital bliss."

MARITAL BLISS

We all want it. We dreamed of it before marriage and thought we'd achieve it after saying I do. The problem is we don't really know what marital bliss looks like or how to get it. We try a myriad of methods only to come up short. The Word of God has help for us. Amazingly, the book of Genesis offers three benchmarks of marital bliss: perfection, priority, and partnership.

> We don't really know what marital
> bliss looks like or how to get it.

PERFECTION

In Genesis 2 we find a place of perfection: the Garden of Eden. This garden had everything Adam and Eve needed. Their physical needs were completely satisfied. Their emotional needs were completely fulfilled. God was the complete supplier of it all. They were in perfect relationship with their heavenly Father as He walked with them in the cool of the day. It was marital bliss in a perfect place.

Sure, we don't live in Eden anymore, and there are no perfect marriages. But that doesn't mean we shouldn't strive for it. Just as Paul asks in Romans 6:1-2, do we continue in sin because of the abundance of grace freely given? The answer of course is no. We should strive for perfection in our marriages. We won't reach perfection until our glorification but until then we can press on toward that goal (see Philippians 3:14). If you strive for perfection, you might obtain excellence.

So how do imperfect people strive for a perfect marriage? They follow a perfect Savior who supernaturally transforms them through His workmanship toward perfection. When a marriage is grounded on the perfect life of Christ, excellence can be achieved. And this is a goal worth striving for. Are you striving for perfection in your relationship with Christ? With your spouse?

PRIORITY

Secondly, the marriage of Adam and Eve held a place of priority. Genesis 2:24 provides the marriage principle of "leave and cleave." The word *cleave* comes from the Hebrew word *dabag*, which means "to cling or adhere to."[1] It's like taking two pieces of wood, bonding them together with glue, and further attaching them with screws for good measure. They're so connected that to separate them would literally destroy both pieces.

This is why God says He hates divorce (see Malachi 2:16). He knows the covenant marriage He ordained with a man and a woman is one that so binds them together that separating the two will destroy them both. This is why I (Dale) weighed only 145 pounds and Jena only 97 by the end of the divorce. As we separated in heart we destroyed ourselves from the inside out. God created the marriage relationship to be a priority. The reality is that we often make our extended family, children, friends, jobs, or even church the priority of our lives. Next to our relationship with Him, God created the marriage between a man and a woman as the foremost relational priority in our lives. When we view our marriage as top priority, we honor God's ordained design for marital bliss.

> God created the marriage
> relationship to be a priority.

PARTNERSHIP

Finally, the marriage of Adam and Eve formed a partnership. They were united in spirit, soul, and body. A partnership includes two people who share both triumphs and troubles. Genesis 2:24 puts it this way: "they will become one flesh."

In the beginning, God created the heavens and the earth and declared everything good. Yet, after creating Adam, something was still missing. God said it wasn't good for the man to be alone and there was no suitable helpmate for him (see Genesis 2:18). So God created Eve to be Adam's partner in life. Whether you have a partner in golf, business, or Bible study, you understand that what we do, we do together for one common goal, embracing the good and the bad. The same is true in marriage.

Sadly, we find ourselves treating our golf, business, or Bible study partner better than we do our own spouse. Partnership in marriage means that you and your spouse join hand-in-hand on your specifically ordained journey with God. Any decision you make should be made together with your God-ordained marriage partnership as the focus.

> Partnership in marriage means that you and your spouse join hand-in-hand on your specifically ordained journey with God.

Ultimately, partnership in marriage includes spending time in prayer, seeking the face of God, and asking Him to lead your marriage (see Philippians 4:6).

1. When faced with the thought of a perfect marriage, what is your initial reaction? Circle the best answer.

- There's no way, so why try?
- I've never thought about it.
- Sounds like a lot of work.
- I'm willing to try.
- Let's go!

2. Match each kind of perfection from Philippians 3:12-14.

"that for which Christ Jesus took hold of me" (verse 12)	ultimate perfection
"I press on to take hold of" (verse 12)	spiritual maturity
"the goal to win the prize" (verse 14)	positional perfection

3. What kind of glue characterizes your marriage partnership? Circle the best answer.

- Post-it note glue
- Glue-stick glue
- Glitter glue
- Wood glue
- Super glue

4. How does your spouse know he or she is a priority?

5. What's one way you could press on toward spiritual maturity together?

6. According to John 14:16-17, what partner has God given you to help you make your marriage perfect and prioritized?

When a marriage is founded on the perfect life of Christ, both husband and wife make each other a priority. They demonstrate genuine partnership and wrap their lives in prayer. That marriage will experience marital bliss by God's design.

MARITAL BUST

> Lord, I want my marriage to be centered on Your perfection. I want to make my marriage a wonderful partnership. So I ask You to show me where things have gone awry and lead us back to Your truth. In Jesus' name, Amen.

Six months later we met the couple mentioned at the beginning of this chapter. They were sitting in a couples' Sunday school class. When asked how married life was going, the wife responded, "This is not what I bargained for!" Somewhere between two weeks and six months, they stopped experiencing marital bliss. The bliss was replaced by lost hopes and unfulfilled dreams.

Let's return to Adam and Eve, too. They encountered the serpent. Through his deceit, their marital bliss was gone. What happened in this short period of time to both of these couples? What caused the marital bust?

Genesis 2 and 3 identify three benchmarks of marital bust: shame, blame, and pain. They were at the heart of our divorce and contribute to the breakdown of marriages all over the world. No one sets out for marital bust. We surely didn't. Perhaps if we identify the destructive forces, we can stand guard against them.

> When sin and disobedience enter a relationship, marital bust is inevitable.

SHAME

Scripture clearly indicates that sin entered the world through the disobedience of Adam and Eve. Very simply, when sin and disobedience enter a relationship, marital bust is inevitable. First, it can turn our homes into places of shame. Adam and Eve's sin changed their relationship with God and each other. They became so ashamed they sewed fig leaves together to cover their nakedness. While longing to be like God, nakedness was the only thing they discovered through their newfound wisdom. So often we make choices only to find our impure longings don't turn out the way we intended. Adam and Eve wanted to be wise. Instead, they found shame.

Thankfully, when we sin, God through His Holy Spirit brings conviction. Conviction says, "My behavior was wrong." Satan, on the other hand, floods our hearts with shame. Shame says, "There is something wrong with me." It implies that I'm defective while everyone else is okay. This often contributes to the death of a marriage because it results in two people bound by the Enemy using phrases like "you always" and "you never." Shame keeps people bound in their wrongness so they cannot fulfill the purposes for which God created them.

> Shame keeps people bound in their wrongness so they cannot fulfill the purposes for which God created them.

BLAME

If shaming doesn't help us feel better about ourselves, we resort to blame. Adam and Eve blamed one another and even God for their own sin. This is the first time we see the strategy of passing the buck. Have you ever blamed God or your spouse for your situation when it was your own disobedience that caused the problem? Eve blamed the serpent and we do the same thing. Look at these blaming phrases:

- I wouldn't have done that if you hadn't done what you did!
- You made me do that!
- I was just reacting to what you said!

Truthfully, we choose how we'll respond whether it's through blaming others or taking responsibility for our own sin. Nobody can make you do anything. Your behavior is a result of your own choices.

PAIN

There were consequences for Adam and Eve's shaming and blaming. Their sin would last a lifetime, and it certainly involved pain. We've heard it said, "Choose to sin, choose to suffer." One truth about sin is that it will take you farther than you ever intended to go and keep you longer than you ever intended to stay.

If you've ever cut your finger, you've experienced pain. If a scab forms, healing takes place. But if the cut continues to be reopened and never given appropriate time to heal, then you experience chronic pain.

During our first marriage and divorce, we used cutting words that went deep and marred one another. Some of those words left scars that don't hurt too much anymore but are still reminders of where we've been. Still others left deep wounds because they were reopened often as the shaming and blaming continued. The recurring infliction of pain damages the soul. Only the miraculous grace of God can repair the damage.

> The recurring infliction of pain damages the soul.

7. How does Satan convince you to be ashamed?

8. When are you most likely to blame your spouse?

9. What do you think causes this blaming?

10. According to Isaiah 59:2, how does sin affect your relationship with God?

Once sin entered the garden with all its shame, blame, and pain, it separated man from God. Adam and Eve suffered great consequences for their sin, but the ultimate consequence was the void left in their hearts through separation from their heavenly Father. Though Adam and Eve desperately desired to be back in close fellowship with God, there was a vast chasm between them, requiring a unique bridge. God provided that bridge through His Son, Jesus Christ.

WHY AM I SO NEEDY?

Just as Adam and Eve were separated from God, we've allowed sin to separate us from God, the only one who completely fills us and gives us purpose and

> Father God, help me answer this question honestly. In Jesus' name, Amen.

meaning in life. This separation leaves us feeling empty. This void leaves us with big needs. We long to be complete, whole, and in perfect relationship with others. That was God's plan, but because of our separation, we're in need. Often, we will do whatever it takes to have our needs met because we hunger so deeply for their fulfillment.

All of us are aware that we have needs. These needs are legitimate, but many times we're not wise in our choices of whom or what should meet them. The first year of our marriage we noticed how much we needed one another to feel complete and whole. Frustration and bitterness grew as we tried to get each other to fill the insatiable void within our hearts.

> We're not wise in our choices of whom
> or what should meet our needs.

I (Jena) entered our marriage with a need to hear the words "I love you" and "You're so pretty." To me, those words indicated unconditional love, acceptance, and trust. Dale was so young and oblivious to my needs. When I asked him why he never said those things he answered, "When I cease to love you and when I no longer think you're pretty, I'll let you know." That only discouraged me and drove me further in my quest for fulfillment.

EVE'S CURSE

Because of her sin, Eve was left with a quest to fill her neediness. Genesis 3:16 shares the curse of pain in childbirth. Many mothers have experienced this pain, so identifying this firsthand is not a problem. However, the last part of the verse provides insight that revolutionized our marriage. It says, "Your desire will be for your husband, and he will rule over you." The word desire comes from the Hebrew word *tshuwqah* (tesh-oo-kaw), which means "a deep longing for, a craving."[2] When sin entered the world, Eve no longer knew a secure and intimate relationship with God. She was left with a void that longed to be filled. Eve craved Adam in order to get her needs met. When he couldn't fully do so, she tried to rule over him. We call this nagging. As she demanded that her needs be met, incapable Adam would fail. As a result, she became more disappointed and demanding.

As with Eve, women have a deep longing that needs filling. A woman's greatest need in her life is to develop deep intimacy through a safe and secure relationship. She wants to know she is deeply loved and nothing she does, nothing she is or is not, will change that love. She also wants to be confident in the commitment of the one with whom she has a relationship. She wants to know that no matter what happens, her husband is committed to her. While the need for deep intimacy and security is not exclusive to women, it's the primary need of most women. There is no earthly relationship that can fully meet that need.

> God hand-carved the need for intimacy and security in your life so you would see your need for Him.

Women, God hand-carved the need for intimacy and security in your life so you would see your need for Him. Praise God, He sent Jesus to fill your void. If someone or something else could fill that void, Jesus' death would have been in vain. When we look to other things to fulfill us, we make a mockery of Jesus Christ and His death on the cross. We also elevate someone else to a position that belongs to Jesus. This is idolatry, and Christ will share His glory with no one.

Jesus Christ is the only One who can fully meet your need. Men, this doesn't get you off the hook! For every curse there is a calling. Men, now that you know your wife's deepest need is for intimacy, safety, and security, you possess the wonderful privilege of pointing her to the very One who can fulfill that need. By doing so, you enhance freedom in the life of your wife. You free her from demanding what she needs from you or others. You free her from being disappointed when nothing else satisfies. You also free yourself from living a defeated lifestyle. All those times when you did your very best to meet your wife's needs and it was never good enough are past. You never have to feel like a failure. What an awesome calling for men to lead their wives to the unconditional love of Jesus Christ!

11. Which of these describes how you feel about God's love for you? Circle the best answer.

- He loves me no matter what.
- He loves me most of the time.
- I wish I knew He loved me.

12. Read Romans 8:38-39, and then write it in your own words below.

13. According to Jeremiah 31:3, how has God loved you?

14. What does Ephesians 2:13 say about the benefit you gain from this love?

Through Jesus, God wants to fill the void that sin left. Jesus' death paid the penalty for our sin. His blood covers our sin so we can come near to God and our needs can be totally filled. His commitment proved true all the way to the cross. His love is so unconditional that nothing you do or don't do will change His love for you. He wants to fill you to overflowing with His love so His love will pour through you into a world that desperately needs it. How it must break the heart of God to offer His only beloved Son to meet our deepest needs and watch us shun this gift while searching for what we think is better.

Will you allow God to fill every crevice of your heart with His love and commitment to you? This decision will totally and radically change your life and marriage.

ADAM'S CURSE

15. Write your own prayer to God, asking Him to affirm His truth in you.

Meet Jake. Jake worked for months building a deck. He was building it for his family to enjoy. Jake had visions of late-afternoon cookouts with friends and family, watching his children play in the yard, and sitting in the morning, drinking coffee with his wife. This wasn't just a deck; it was a monument of Jake's dedication to his family and his internal sense of accomplishment.

The day of unveiling arrived. Jake invited friends and family and put scrumptious food on the grill. As everyone arrived, Jake proudly escorted them to the deck. The compliments were abundant, yet something was missing. As others raved about the new deck, Jake's wife remained silent. He never received the affirmation from the one he wanted it from the most: his wife.

At the end of the day, Jake shared his hurt feelings with his wife, Tammy. "Everyone was happy for me and made me feel special except you. You could care less about what I do for you or this family! Does anything I do for you really matter?"

What does this show about how couples treat each other? As wonderful as the compliments were from all of Jake's friends and family, he most wanted to hear praise from Tammy. Of all the people Jake wanted to impress, Tammy was at the top of the list. When that didn't happen, Jake was hurt and felt insignificant.

A man's greatest need is to be important. He needs to feel he makes a difference. He hates the thought of living an invisible, weightless life. He may have a tough outward appearance, but the truth is he still has a deep need to leave his mark and accomplish something with his life. And when they accomplish it, they long to be recognized for it.

Just as Eve was cursed for her sin, so was Adam. His curse involved the sweating and toiling of work (see Genesis 3:17-19). And with that curse came a root need that is evident in every man: the need for importance. Adam lost his position of importance as king of Eden. He wanted to feel that importance in position once again. Husbands, if you've ever been frustrated at your attempts to succeed, you can identify with the pain of feeling unimportant. In the arena of marriage, feelings of insignificance can lead to marital bust. You try to do things that will please your wife. When they go unnoticed or they don't please her, you feel defeated.

Praise God, you were never created with the capacity to fully meet your wife's needs! It's easy to fall into this spiral: try, fail, feel defeated; try, fail, feel defeated. Keep this up, and you'll quit trying altogether and shut down emotionally. No man with the innate need to feel valued and important will put himself continually in positions to fail. But men, just as with a woman's need for intimacy, no earthly relationship can fully meet a man's need for importance.

God left the void in your life so that you
would let Him fill that need with Himself.

Men, God left the void in your life so that you would let Him fill that need with Himself. He longs to strengthen you in the deepest recesses of your heart. Unfortunately, guys stuff their hearts with all the wrong things. We focus on work, money, bigger houses, nicer cars, sports, trophies, or even other relationships to find our importance. Jesus Christ is the only one who can satisfy the deep longing in your soul to find importance and worth. He created you with a specific purpose.

Her senior year in high school, Jena was in a horrible automobile accident. She was rushed to the emergency room where her mother stood over Jena's bed and made this simple but life-changing statement: "God left you on this earth for a purpose. You'd best find out what it is and do it with all of your heart." Friend, God has a plan for your life. He has left you on this earth for a purpose. You'd best find out what it is and do it with all of your heart.

Women, don't think that this gets you off the hook! With this curse on the men comes a calling for you as well. You have the privilege of pointing your husband to the One who made him important in the first place. It is imperative that your husband knows you appreciate what he does for you and your family, but more importantly that God sees great value in him. Don't miss the opportunity to be grateful by verbally recognizing your husband's hard work and sacrifice for you. But more than that, point him to the very One who can give him spiritual value and direction—Jesus Christ.

16. How do you feel after reading this? Circle the best answer.

- If God has a plan, I don't have a clue what it is.
- God has a plan for my life, and I'm going to start seeking it out.
- I'm fulfilling the purpose for which God made me.

17. What does Luke 12:24 say about your importance to God?

18. According to Jeremiah 29:11, what meaningful plans does God have for you?

19. Read Ecclesiastes 2:17-26. Based on verses 24-25, what is the key turning point from meaningless to meaningful toil?

Once you realize that chasing after *things* won't meet your needs for intimacy and importance, you will turn to the authentic *need meeter*, Jesus. From the moment of your creation, God had plans for you. And His plans are for your good. There isn't a single bird that falls to the ground that our Father doesn't know about. How much more important are you to Him than a bird?

You were created with a great purpose. Will you commit yourself to seek God's intimate and important purpose for your life? Will you let Him fill your void? Make yourself available for His plans and you'll begin an incredible journey with your Savior.

VICIOUS CYCLE

Invite the Holy Spirit to show you how to apply this truth to your life and marriage.

We've come to recognize our needs for intimacy and importance as individuals and discovered how Christ is the only one who can meet those needs. When we seek other ways to meet our needs, we get caught in a vicious cycle that too many times spins out of control.

....

When we seek other ways to meet our
needs, we get caught in a vicious cycle that
too many times spins out of control.

....

Our marriage was a perfect example. Jena wanted to be needed and loved. When I (Dale) didn't meet that need, she went to church and taught a Bible study. The women in the study loved her and needed her. Jena spent so much time with those women that I felt demoted on Jena's scale of importance. So I headed to the golf course, where I attempted to win every match to feel better about myself. Jena realized I was spending more time at the golf course than with her, so she felt less intimacy and security. She poured her life into singing and writing musicals. I assumed I wasn't important to her anymore, so I headed to the office to climb the corporate ladder where everyone acknowledged my efforts and affirmed my good work. The cycle continued. Jena recalls thinking during her pregnancy, *When Dale sees the pain I go through to give him a son, he'll love me more.*

What measures we took to fulfill our own needs!

Broken and shattered, our divorce taught us that all we had was Jesus and that He was all we needed. His love, goodness, and presence are the only things that can fill the deep needs of our lives and make us healthy and whole. As we allowed Him to fill our empty hearts, we were able to minister to one another. No more empty hearts, no more empty home.

FREEDOM: STOPPING THE CYCLE

As a child, I (Jena) would have said that the icing was the best part of the cake. As an adult, the best part has become the cake. Icing just happens to be a little sweet extra that comes along with the cake.

As Dale and I allow Christ to fill the neediness in our lives, we no longer starve for intimacy and importance from each other. When Christ filled those areas in our lives, He became the foundation or the "cake" of our hearts. The affirmation, love, and acceptance we receive from each other are wonderful and welcomed, but it's not what we stake our lives on. Instead, it's a nice addition to the fullness we already experience in and through Christ. Our favorite part has become the cake, and the icing we receive from one another is just the sweet added extra.

You can be free from the demands of your mate's neediness when you agree to allow Christ to meet their needs. You just offer extra encouragement. You can be free from disappointment when your mate is not meeting your needs because you no longer expect them to be the primary person who meets your needs. They are the icing on the cake. And you're free from feelings of defeat that come when your mate doesn't meet your expectations. When both you and your spouse are daily filling yourselves with Christ you can each be free to love, encourage, and affirm your spouse out of devotion, not out of duty. Doesn't that sound like freedom to you?

Shame, blame, and pain took us down a road toward marital bust we never dreamed we'd travel. If you've found that your marriage is not what you bargained for, see if the characteristics of marital bust have found a place to lodge in your heart. Ask your heavenly Father to tear down those areas that have crept into your life. Let God do His continuing work in your life and the life of your spouse. Ground your marriage in the elements of marital bliss founded on the perfect life of Christ. You can be confident in His work as you allow Him to refine you. Then your relationship can be above and beyond what you could have ever imagined. That's God's desire for us.

20. Beside each Scripture, write what God says about our needs.

2 Corinthians 9:8

Philippians 4:19

Hebrews 4:16

Galatians 5:1 says, "It is for freedom that Christ has set us free." Christ came to set you free from sin and from death and from the neediness of one another. Christ set you free so you can freely minister in love to one another because your needs have been filled by Him. No more empty hearts resulting in empty homes.

THE WEEK IN ACTION

Let's take some time to evaluate ourselves and our marriage in light of what we have learned.

21. What is the root need of women?

22. What is the root need of men?

23. On the line below, put a G where your neediness from God is and an S where your neediness from your spouse is.

|—————————————————————————————————|

Not Needy at All   Very Needy

24. What does this say to you about your neediness?

25. What might God be saying to you about your needs?

Higher-Risk Option: Based on where you are relationally, ask your spouse where he or she sees your neediness showing the most. Remember: Don't ask if you don't want to know. If you ask, accept what he or she says. Ask your spouse for some tangible ways you could better let Christ meet your needs. Ask him or her to partner with you as you seek to have your needs met by Christ. (For example, if you're going to work on spending time each morning with God in His Word, they could make sure the house is quiet and you're uninterrupted during that time or they could join you in prayer as you look to Him in all things.)

As you begin your personal journey, allow Christ to fill all your needs. You'll be setting your spouse free from the burden of perfectly meeting them every time, as well as freeing yourself. You'll be filled and able to minister to the needs of your spouse and others around you who need to see Jesus through you.

EMPTY HEARTS, EMPTY HOMES

Luke 9:10-17; Mark 6:30-44;
Matthew 14:15-21—The Feeding of the 5,000

Jesus used the _____ to explain the _____.

Marriage Bliss Principle #1: _____ **your need**
(Luke 9:10-11).

Wherever a need is _____, the Lord is ready to

_____ it.

Guard against _____. "I have the strength."

Marriage Bliss Principle #2: _____
your need (Mark 6:30-44).

Guard against _____ and _____.

Marriage Bliss Principle #3: _____

_____ **your need** (Matthew 14:15-21).

Recognize that God _____ the need, and He wants to

_____ it.

Yet often, He allows you to be a _____ of it.

Guard against _____ because it erodes

_____.

Marriage Bliss Principle #4: _____

God's supply to others (Philippians 4:19; Psalm 119).

Guard against _____. "I am the source."

Now turn to appendix A (page 177) and write down your resolution.

Chapter Four

A LOOK AT OUR LEGACY

His mercy extends to those who fear him, from generation to generation.

Luke 1:50

When we married the first time, we had no clue what we were getting into. At the ages of twenty-one and twenty-two, we just knew we loved each other, everybody else was getting married, and so were we. We didn't know much about each other's lives

> Lord of life, please show me the abundant life You offer for me and my marriage and how the Enemy has attempted to sabotage it. In Jesus' name, Amen.

before marriage and how our enemy, Satan, operated. We had no idea the Enemy used the formational years of our lives, the homes we were raised in, the experiences we had, and the life we lived before getting married to attack our relationship.

THE ENEMY

Whether you believe it or not, you have an enemy who is against you and your marriage. His only goal is utter ruin for you and your home, and he'll stop at nothing until he reaches that goal. Don't lose heart. Remember that God's Word promises us we are overcomers through Jesus Christ, our Lord.

> You have an enemy who is against
> you and your marriage.

In John 10:10 God's Word tells us that the thief, Satan, comes to steal, kill, and destroy. Have you ever thought about what it is that he's trying to kill, steal, and destroy? Scripture tells us God holds us in the palm of His righteous right hand. Nothing can pluck us out of it (see John 10:28). So what does Satan want to steal, kill, or destroy from a Christian couple? It's the abundant life Christ offers. If you're a child of the King, Satan will do whatever he can to steal your joy, kill your passion, and destroy your marriage. A Christ-centered marriage is the picture of Christ's relationship as the Bridegroom to His church, the bride (see Ephesians 5:31-32). Satan knows if you get the marriage relationship right, there are generations to follow that will also get it right.

THE ENEMY'S STRATEGY

Once we learned about our root needs of intimacy and importance, we began to see how Satan attacked our minds. He deceived us into thinking that things other than Christ could meet our needs and fill the voids in our lives.

Lies, facades of intimacy, and accusations are the way of the Enemy. He lies to us about who we are and who God is. He is like a scheming snake, seeking ways to divide and destroy us. This is why we're told in Ephesians 6:11, "Put on the full armor of God so that you can take your stand against the devil's schemes." So while Satan doesn't deserve our focus and attention, we shouldn't underestimate or ignore his plots against the children of God.

> We shouldn't underestimate or ignore
> Satan's plots against the children of God.

We believe that the Enemy's strategy works something like this: We enter the world with needs. The Enemy deceives us into thinking that other people or things will meet those needs. We exchange the truth that Christ will meet our needs for the Enemy's lies. Proverbs 23:7 says, "As he thinks in his heart, so is he" (NKJV). As we think wrong thoughts, we begin to behave in ways that reflect our belief in the lie. Before we know it, Satan has a stronghold in our lives. We are slaves to the never-ending quest to fill our needs and are no longer free to enjoy the abundant life God has planned for us. The diagram below depicts the path the Enemy uses.

Needs *lead to* → Deception *leads to* → Lies *lead to* →

Behavior *leads to* → Stronghold

Maybe the lie you've accepted as truth is, "If I could just make a little more money, then I'd feel important and valuable around here." Or maybe it's, "If I could just look like that movie star, then I'd be loved and accepted." These are lies that can consume you and your behavior. They become your focus, and you lose sight of God. Remember, the Enemy is after the abundant life offered by Christ. He wants you to be blinded to what your heavenly Father wants to give you.

1. Write down the three things the thief comes to do, according to John 10:10.

2. When has the Enemy tried to do this to you? To your marriage?

3. Describe what the abundant life that Jesus is offering might look like.

4. Think of what you've been missing because of our Enemy's schemes! List the descriptions of the Enemy found in the Scripture verses below.

John 8:44

1 Peter 5:8

5. Looking back at the Enemy's strategy, where might he have lied and sought to devour you?

GETTING TO THE ROOT

6. Write a prayer to the Lord, asking Him to reveal where the Enemy has stolen some joy or killed some passion. Finish your prayer by thanking Him for loving you enough to reveal the lies so that you can experience the freedom and abundant life He offers in your marriage.

As we share how we were raised, the influences in our lives before we married, and the lies the Enemy used in our lives to neutralize our marriage, we pray that the Spirit of God will reveal lies that may have been passed down to you. This isn't a parent-bashing chapter, nor should it degrade your family heritage. God's Word tells us to honor our parents (see Exodus 20:12). Your family may have wonderful attributes, but they may also have some less admirable characteristics. The goal is to see how the Enemy has lied to us, remove these lies from our lives, and replace them with the truth of God's Word. Isn't it an incredible thought that God can use you to defeat the lies that have held your family captive? This is why Christ came, that you might know Him and His truth so you would be free (see John 8:32; Luke 4:18-19).

> Isn't it an incredible thought that God
> can use you to defeat the lies that
> have held your family captive?

Jena's grandparents lived on a farm in Georgia. She loved to watch her grandparents farm all the fruits and vegetables. She learned how an apple can reflect Satan's attack on our lives. From a flower bud on an apple tree, an apple will form. Many times, however, a worm attaches itself to the flower bud. The fruit of the apple grows around the bud. So when you see a hole in an apple, its not that the worm has worked its way in but that it has worked its way out! This happens to us. The Enemy, like a worm, has attached a lie to the bud of our hearts, even as children. The fruit (behavior) of our lives has grown around that lie.

We try various methods to fix or clean the fruit of our lives. We work on communication or problems with anger, depression, eating disorders, performance, and perfectionism. While it's noble to work on these things, life change will rarely occur until we deal with the root of our problems. Many of these behaviors are fruit that comes from a worm attached to the bud in our lives or even our family line.

> ### Life change will rarely occur until we deal with the root of our problems.

> Holy Spirit, reveal to me the lies I haven't seen so I can bear better fruit. In Jesus' name, Amen.

JENA'S LIE: THE 99 SYNDROME

I (Jena) grew up in a loving home with wonderful Christian parents who taught me the value of church, servanthood, and commitment. I was confident that God would provide, because my parents worked hard and sacrificed for me. From an early age, though, I felt I wasn't good enough. When I made a 99 on a math test, I knew it should've been 100. Feeling my parents would be disappointed, I struggled to be the best. Still, I was just a 99—not quite good enough.

The Enemy fueled these thoughts with condemnation about my less-than-acceptable and less-than-perfect life. I began questioning God and His love for me. I bought the lie that I wasn't good enough. I remember losing my best friend to a new girl at school. The Enemy taunted my thinking: "You're just not good enough. Even your friends think so!" The one beauty pageant I entered, I was awarded Miss Congeniality. The deceptive voice of Satan cried out, "Jena, you're not quite good enough. That's why you didn't win." I remember striving to graduate number one in my class and being number nine. I needed the approval of others and God, so I did whatever anybody wanted me to do. Though I worked hard and gained the approval of some, I was miserable on the inside, exhausted from the struggle. The 99 Syndrome held me captive for twenty-seven years.

DALE'S LIE: THE COMPETITOR'S SYNDROME

I (Dale) grew up in a Christian home where I was taught the value of church, hard work, and fairness. I'm also an identical twin. So I was never my own person. I quickly learned the importance of being number one. I fought for my own identity. I felt if I was better at everything, that my accomplishments would make me valuable. So I competed to be number one in baseball, basketball, golf, girls, grades, and popularity. The Enemy took advantage of this competitive quest to lie to me. I bought the lie that I had to be the best at everything (or at least be better than my twin brother) to be valuable and important. This carried over into my view of God. I thought I had to compete for God's love— to be perfect and successful, to be loved and accepted by Him. The result was a hard-charging husband with an unhealthy need for approval. Jena found herself married to a man wrapped up in a stronghold of self-sufficiency that I call the Competitor's Syndrome.

I bought into the lie that I had to be the best at everything in order to be valuable and important.

7. Read the following passages and write down the connection between the roots and the results.

Romans 11:16

Matthew 12:33

Matthew 13:6; 13:21

Perhaps you identify with our lies or there's a different lie you've accepted as truth from Satan. Here's a list of potential lies and strongholds in your life:

- I must be perfect to be loved.
- I'm unloved, unworthy, unacceptable.
- I'm inadequate, with nothing to offer.
- My past is too dark to ever be free from it.
- There's nothing special about me.
- I'll always be this way.
- I don't need anyone; the only thing I need is me.
- God may work for you, but not for me.

Maybe you believe the only way to be accepted is to look pretty, so you're trapped by anorexia or bulimia. Maybe you're addicted to food, alcohol, or another substance. Perhaps you learned at an early age that possessions bring happiness, so you're totally dependent on what you own. Right now, pray for God to reveal the lies so you can uproot them. When Jesus replants His truth in your life, you'll no longer be held hostage.

STUDYING YOUR FAMILY TREE

Lies from Satan give us an unhealthy view of ourselves and God. Our family histories also profoundly affect how we relate to others. Studying our families helped us identify the struggles we had in our marriage. It also helped us see wonderful Christlike characteristics that we wanted to pass to future generations. Much of what we saw was neither right nor wrong, it was just different. Those differences caused some major issues for us. Once we realized our differences, we better understood each other and how to work through them. We began by drawing our family trees from our grandparents down to ourselves.

Jena's Family Tree

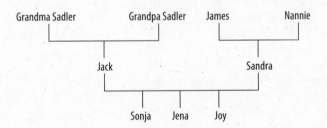

Dale's Family Tree

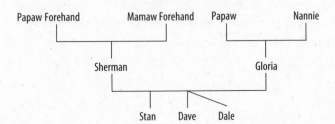

8. In the space below, draw your family tree. Yours may look different. The goal is for you to insert the people who most influenced your life and upbringing.

Lord, You know me. You created me. You placed me in the family that would best mold me and prepare me for fulfilling the purposes for which I was created. I honor my parents and grandparents and am grateful for them. I also know they were not perfect, nor am I. I pray that You would reveal the areas in my family line You want me to pass on to future generations, as well as areas that You want to be removed. Help me to be the one who digs up negative roots so my marriage can grow and those who come behind me will not be held captive to those areas anymore. In Jesus' name, Amen.

After drawing our family tree, we wrote the characteristics of each person on the tree. Their impact on us, communication patterns, responses to conflict or stress, and repeated patterns of behavior were just a few things we recorded. We began to see how many coping mechanisms and attitudes had been passed down to us. Some of these qualities and characteristics were causing some differences and conflicts between us. Neither person's upbringing was better, right or wrong, they were just different. The Enemy loves to enhance our differences to drive a wedge in our relationship.

....

The Enemy loves to enhance our differences
to drive a wedge in our relationship.

....

9. Circle the characteristics you've inherited or learned in your life. Put
a + next to the ones you consider positive and a – next to the negative
ones. Neutral ones don't need a sign.

Abusive	Flexible	Private
Affectionate	Giver	Private spiritually
Affirming	Happy-go-lucky	Quiet and reserved
Agreeable	Humble	Rebellious
Angry	Impulsive	Rigid
Antichurch	Internal processor	Saver
Antisocial	Loud and outgoing	Self-centered
Avoids conflict	Manipulative	Servant-hearted
Caretaker	Matter-of-fact	Social
Church attendee	Nonaffectionate	Spender
Clown	Nonengaging	Teachable
Dictator	Open	Touchy-feely
Distant	Open conflict	Workaholic
Engaging	Open spiritually	Other _____
External processor	Peacemaker	Other _____

10. Who influenced you the most as a child? How are you like and
unlike that person?

11. How did you see conflict handled? What was the resolve, if any? How did you react to it?

12. How did you see your parents or guardians interact with each other? How much time did they spend together?

OUR FAMILY TREES

Offer a prayer of gratitude to the Lord for what He has shown you. Ask Him to help you accentuate the positives and work toward tearing out the negatives, replacing them with His life and character.

JENA'S TREE

My paternal grandparents were greatly work-oriented and carried high levels of commitment regarding both church and family. They taught my father to know and love God's Word and to be active and committed to the church. My grandfather loved Coke and peanuts and always had them for our family when we visited. He loved a good laugh. My father grew into a hard worker with strong commitments, who was funny and a wonderful provider. He was a product of how he was raised.

My maternal grandparents were very service-oriented. They were friendly and social. They lived on a farm and helped many needy people in their community. Both of them died during our divorce, which confronted me with the certainty of death and the brevity of life. At their funerals, people I didn't know came up to me, sharing what my grandparents had done for them. During their lives, they received no accolades or applause. They loved as Christ loves. Because of them, my mother is a loving, fun, affectionate, giving person. What a sobering thought: Our children become what they see daily.

What a sobering thought: Our children become what they see daily.

My parents handled conflict by talking it out until it was resolved. Their motto was "Don't let the sun go down on your wrath." They worked hard at a resolution, even if it took all night. They also spent the majority of their time together.

So I came into marriage believing that I was a 99, confident that I would always be provided for, and willing to give and serve when I saw a need. I also shared my parents' value of laughter and loving God's Word. I thought that everything should be talked out and that Dale and I should spend all of our time together. After all, that's what happened in my home and everybody's home looked the same, right?

DALE'S TREE

My paternal grandparents were all about ministry. My grandfather was a Baptist preacher, committed to ministering to others. Many people told me how he spoke the Word of God boldly and unashamedly. Today I share his heartbeat to preach and teach the Word in ministry to others.

My father was the oldest of five children, so he felt responsible for leadership and keeping peace in the home in his father's absence. My father was the ultimate peacemaker.

My maternal grandparents were the hardest working people in America. They married during the height of the Depression and learned the value of hard work and partnership. They were service-oriented and giving. I loved playing in my grandmother's backyard and having candy waiting for me when I got off the school bus. The attention she gave me made me feel I was the most important person in the world. My mother became a hard-working and giving person, just like her parents. She showed her love through service to her children just as her mother had.

My parents brought their histories into their marriage. I never saw conflict in my home because my father was a peacemaker. My parents worked hard during the week, so they spent the weekends doing things they enjoyed, such as playing golf and serving the family. Many times they simply did their own thing.

Can you see the similarities of faith and family priority in the ways we were raised? Can you also see how differently we were raised? When we realized these differences we gained a completely different perspective of our marriage. Jena came, needing affirmation that told her "You're a 100," "You're beautiful," "I love you." She expected to talk through our conflict and spend most of our time together. I came into the marriage needing to feel valued and important. I also desired physical affection from Jena. I did whatever it took to keep the peace and wanted time away to do my own thing. Can you see why we had struggles in our marriage?

Joined Together

Our first year of marriage was difficult as we tried to get the other to meet our needs. When conflict arose, Jena wanted to talk things out while Dale wanted to go to bed, hoping tomorrow would be better. When I (Dale) went to bed, it told Jena she must be a 99, because if I really loved her I would stay up and talk it out. How sad that I had no idea what I was communicating! I was working hard to provide for my family and keep the peace.

Early on, we had a major disagreement. As the fight escalated, I (Dale) went to bed. This was how I sought to keep peace. Frustrated, Jena left the house. She drove around until 2 a.m. When she returned home, I was fast asleep. For someone who thought she was a 99, I affirmed the lie. What did Jena want me to do? She wanted me to summon the police, call her parents, wake the pastor, send out the bloodhounds, and do whatever it took to find her. Why? Because she was worth it! She wanted to know I valued her as my "100" bride and gift from God. When that didn't occur, the pain was intense, the lie confirmed, and the stronghold reinforced.

It wasn't that Jena's ways were right and mine wrong or vice versa. They were simply different. Our ignorance of our family dynamics caused injured feelings, captivity to the Enemy's lies, and strongholds of behaviors. Now when conflicts arise, I (Jena) know I want to talk them out, but I also know that Dale needs time to think about it. So to minister to each other, I offer Dale the time he needs. He suggests a time when we can talk it out. We're taking our differences and ministering to each other rather than demanding our own way.

IN YOUR MARRIAGE

How has the Enemy been holding your marriage captive to his lies? How has your family of origin affected your marriage? When the Holy Spirit shines His light into our lives we are set free from the dark, hidden areas and the deceptive lies of the Enemy. John 1:4-5 says, "In him was life, and that life was the light of men. The light shines in the darkness, but the darkness has not understood it." The darkness cannot overcome the light. Christ lived a life that was a light for us to live by. Freedom comes from walking in the light of Christ.

For some, digging deep into the recesses of your hearts and homes may be easy. For others, it may be a tough and painful experience. Facing a difficult and painful past is never easy. Yet to be set free, we must remove the bad roots that are bearing bad fruit in our marriage. Is it possible? We hope you've been encouraged by seeing how God released us from the Enemy's snare. The only requirement was to cooperate with God through obedience.

13. Read these Scriptures and record the most important words or phrases as they apply to your freedom.

2 Peter 1:3-10

Romans 8:25-28

Lord Jesus, thank You for these promises. Holy Spirit, please intercede on my behalf. Bring me freedom for my life and marriage. Thank You for working everything for Your good. Help me to cooperate with You and allow You to help me tear down the strongholds in my life. Help me to uproot them and replace them with Your truth so that my life and marriage can be all that You intend. In Jesus' name, Amen.

TEARING DOWN THE STRONGHOLDS

As we discovered the lies and sought to destroy them, God took us on a path toward healing and wholeness through close communion with the Holy Spirit. He showed us how to tear down the strongholds in our lives. We learned this isn't something you do only once, but as a daily choice as we walk in freedom.

The first thing we had to do was *acknowledge* the lies that held us captive. Just as an alcoholic must admit that there's a problem, we have to admit the lies we've accepted as truth. The Bible urges us to put on the whole armor of God (see Ephesians 6:11), and the first piece of armor is the belt of truth. We have to acknowledge the lies we've accepted so the real truth can take over.

We couldn't do this alone. We weren't designed to. Jesus says, "apart from [Him we] can do nothing" (John 15:5). That's why the next step in the journey to freedom must be an *appeal* to God (see Philippians 4:6-7). God wants us to call out to Him without embellishments. He simply wants our hearts honestly seeking His saving grace and truth. When we were going through our divorce, I (Jena) climbed into the bunk bed every night and cried to the Lord from a wounded heart simply saying, "Help me." These prayers were the most precious prayers ever prayed, for they were from a heart at the end of itself and begging for the Father's help. In the hopeless moments, appeal to your heavenly Father.

After acknowledging our strongholds and appealing to God in prayer, we had to *adopt* a new way of thinking. Picture a recording playing a lie until you've accepted it as truth. Jena continually heard, "You're a 99 and always will be." Jena's expectations grew from her false belief system. My (Dale) lie played continuously saying, "I'll win at any cost." We had to erase the recordings and replace them with truthful ones. This was a process. We'd lived these lies a long time. We had to practice believing and walking in our newfound truth that God had for us.

Jena had to remember she was a 100 plus—not because of anything good in her, but because Christ lives in her life. Dale had to remember he didn't have to be perfect or win to be important. His importance comes from Christ's death on his behalf.

It's time for God's truth to become
your new way of thinking and living.

We didn't know how to begin, so we got up every morning and simply asked God these questions: "What do You think about me? Would You guide me into all truth?" God walked us through the pages of His Word and showed us daily what He thought of us. It's time for God's truth to become your new way of thinking and living.

14. Read the following Scriptures and write down what the Word of God says about you.

Genesis 1:26

Psalm 56:8

Isaiah 43:1-5

Jeremiah 29:11

Matthew 19:26

Philippians 4:13

The words of our Father, Savior, and Friend began to sweep over us and change our outlook and behavior, freeing us from the lies that held us. We found the truth that set us free (see John 8:32). The truth of Christ destroys the Enemy's hold over us. Our adversary is defeated! The blood of Jesus Christ and the word of our testimony defeats him (see Revelation 12:11).

For each of us there's a day of reckoning when you can no longer blame your past or the failures of others. You acknowledge your stronghold, appeal to God in prayer, adopt a new way of thinking, and live in the freedom Christ offers you. Don't let the Enemy direct you anymore. You can be free in Jesus Christ from the lies, the pain of past sin, your past struggles, and your differences. You can glorify Him through your life and marriage. Hallelujah, what a Savior!

THE WEEK IN ACTION

15. As we close this week, take a moment to review the Enemy's strategy. Summarize it here.

16. Write out one lie the Enemy has used in your life.

17. Write a prayer asking God to help you acknowledge and tear down any strongholds.

18. Find a Scripture that speaks directly to your life and your freedom as you adopt God's truth as your truth.

19. How might you get God's truth to take root in your mind and heart?

20. Review your family tree. Write one positive trait that's been passed down to you.

21. Record one negative trait you no longer want to be passed down in your family.

22. What can you do to keep this negative trait from passing down to future generations?

Higher-Risk Option: Based on where you are relationally, you might want to share with one another the lie(s) that the Enemy has used against you and how it has affected your marriage. You might also want to share the positive and negative traits that you discovered in your family tree and how they've affected your marriage. Together seek ways to speak the truth to each other to help you overcome the lie(s) you've lived in. Seek the Lord about how you can work through your differences and partner to break the cycles of generational negative traits.

A LOOK AT OUR LEGACY

Genesis 12–50—From Abraham to Joseph

Abraham is given the promise.
Abraham tells Sarah to lie.
Sarah tries to control situation / Hagar and Ishmael (Islam).
Sarah gives birth to Isaac.

Isaac marries Rebekah / Jacob and Esau.
Jacob lies to Isaac about who he is.
Rebekah tries to control situation / Jacob receives blessing.

Jacob is lied to by Laban in order to get Rachel.
Rachel tries to control situation / Bilhah.
Rachel gives birth to Joseph.

Joseph is lied to by his brothers.
His brothers lie to their father, Jacob.
Joseph lies to his brothers.
Jacob blesses Joseph's younger son instead of firstborn.

Two HUGE Marriage Busters are: _____ **and**
_____ (Proverbs 17:20).

The root is _____.

The result is _____.

The remedy is _____.

1 John 4:11-21—Love is perfected when we:

_____ God's perfect love.

_____ our spouse under God's control.

_____ to our spouse honestly.

The requirement is _____ (1 Corinthians 13:13;
Galatians 5:6).

If we can pass this down to our children and the generations to
follow, we will have a beautiful legacy that lasts an eternity
(Isaiah 59:21).

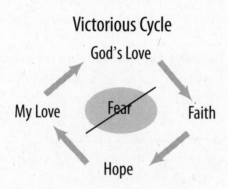

**Now turn to appendix A (page 177) and write down your
resolution.**

Chapter Five

THE SHAME TRAIN

Those who look to him are radiant; their faces are never covered with shame.

Psalm 34:5

During our reconciliation journey, we were amazed at what the Holy Spirit was revealing to us about ourselves, our upbringing, our needs, our motives, and our hearts. Some of it was good, but some of it was despicable. As we began to see the sin that was penetrating our hearts and lives, God gave us a new perspective of ourselves.

> Lord, by the power of Your Holy Spirit, my Friend, Helper, and Revealer of truth, come alongside me and help me surrender every part of my heart to Your redeeming work. In Jesus' name, Amen.

Like uneaten leftovers in our refrigerators, we often allow sin to take up residence in our hearts until it rots. When we allow the Enemy to deceive us with his slant on the sin in our lives, he distorts our way of thinking by flooding our minds with shame.

Shame is a real emotion. It's the feeling that everybody else is normal and okay, but you're not. It's not just that you made mistakes, it says there's something wrong with you—you're defective physically, mentally, or emotionally, believing that everybody else has it all together but you don't. Shame makes you feel that damage has been done to who you are and it can't be repaired.

Shame makes you feel that damage
has been done to who you are
and it can't be repaired.

There's a huge difference between conviction regarding sin and shame from sin. Conviction says, "I made a mistake and need to confess, repent, and move forward with God." Shame says, "I am a mistake. I mess up all the time and I can't get it together. God must be disgusted with me." Conviction draws you deeper in relationship with God while shame keeps you distant from Him. Many of us are rotting in the Devil's snare of shame.

Have you ever thought, "If others really knew me they wouldn't like me"? This signals shame and the Enemy is using it to keep you captive.

Many carry shame from sin that was self-inflicted, sin of their own choosing. Others carry shame from sin someone else inflicted on them. Regardless, shame takes root in your heart and leaves you with stagnant relationships.

Shame takes root in your heart and leaves
you with stagnant relationships.

During our divorce trial, Dale and I accused each other of affairs, child neglect, child abuse, and mental instability. The pain was indescribable. I (Jena) hoped I was dreaming, that we hadn't really said those things. But it was no dream, and the wounds we inflicted were extreme. The Enemy used our assault on each other's hearts to plant seeds of shame deep within us, leaving us wounded and resistant to love or give. I felt I was worthless and ruined for life. These feelings led us down a road that God never intended for us to travel. Dale and I call it the "shame train."

1. How might you describe the difference between shame and conviction?

2. Which of these areas of shame do you believe most people experience? Circle the best answer.

- Shame due to willful disobedient sin
- Shame due to being sinned against
- Some of both

3. How do you think shame affects individuals? Affects a marriage?

4. How might healthy conviction from the Lord affect an individual? Affect a marriage?

5. According to Acts 3:19, what happens when we allow our sin to transform us instead of shame us?

May God help us to not be taken by Satan's snare of shame over our sin or the sin of others.

THE ELEMENTS OF SHAME

Take a moment and ask the Lord to give you strength to walk through His revelation of some shameful areas in your life that you haven't dealt with that may be affecting your life and marriage. Ask Him for courage to face it and comfort to embrace it. Ask this in the name of Jesus.

The shame train looks something like this:

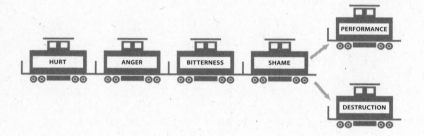

HURT leads to ANGER leads to BITTERNESS leads to SHAME leads to either PERFORMANCE or DESTRUCTION

Willful disobedience and/or being sinned against can leave us very wounded and hurt. If we don't deal with the sin in our lives or the hurt from someone else, shame is right around the corner. Eventually, suppressing it or ignoring it will no longer work. We will be trapped in anger, bitterness, and shame. This is why sometimes we don't even recognize the source of our anger. We're angry for allowing sin into our lives. We're angry with others who might have prevented shameful experiences. We're angry with God for allowing our sinfulness or the sinfulness of others. This leads to bitterness—a ceaseless focus on the hurt. Before we're aware of it, we've become depressed, lifeless, dwelling on the hurt. To cope, our behavior reflects one of two extremes: performing our way into feeling good or self-destruction through anger, control, and manipulation.

I (Jena) chose the road of performance. I'd already bought the Enemy's lie that I was just a 99. Moving from shame to performance as an escape wasn't a big leap. I hoped to perform my way into the hearts of others and God by my personality, intelligence, and appearance. My hopes for happiness soon deteriorated as condemning feelings consumed my thinking. An inner voice kept saying, *There's too much woundedness and sin in my life to have any value.* I was convinced God would always be disappointed in me. I created a false self to cover up who I once was—a new Jena. Just like Adam and Eve, I created my own elaborate fig leaves.

Dale headed toward destruction. Feelings of shame made him come out fighting. His battle cry was, "I'll destroy whoever or whatever is not on my side." He believed that if you're not for me, then you're against me. This response wasn't a big leap since his upbringing and Satan's lies had already trapped him into becoming a highly charged competitive person. He continued on a pendulum path, swinging from forceful control to emotional numbness.

6. Do you relate more to Jena's example or Dale's? Fill in these blanks regarding your own shame train. This takes a lot of courage, so if you're not ready, it's okay to skip this and come back to it later.

I was hurt when I/by . . .

It made me angry because . . .

I recognize bitterness has set in by the way I . . .

I have responded with (circle one or both) performance or destruction in these ways:

7. What does God promise in 1 Peter 5:10-11 as a result of suffering? Circle all that apply.

- To inflict more suffering
- To make you strong
- To make you more angry
- To personally restore you

Take comfort in knowing that God is personally committed to your healing and restoration. His all-surpassing power and grace will grant you healing and strength as you journey through this difficult process with Him.

UNDERSTANDING OUR SHAME

> Pray John 8:32 over your life: "Then you will know the truth, and the truth will set you free."

Shame appears in various forms throughout Scripture. One word that continually appears within its definitions is *confusion*. As we travel on the shame train we forget who God created us to be. We become confused about who we are because we're so consumed by the shame we feel before God and others.

....

We become confused about who we are because we're so consumed by the shame we feel before God and others.

....

Who is the author of confusion? Satan always tries to holds us captive in shame by confusing us about who we are. He causes us to question ourselves and God. Isn't this what he did through his assault on Adam and Eve, causing them to stumble into their sin? He enslaved them through doubt and confusion. In the end, they were ashamed. The Enemy still uses this strategy today, shaming believers into captivity.

Consider a woman who was sexually abused or raped earlier in her life. The hurt that mars her heart puts her on the shame train and she doesn't even know it. She continually struggles with her weight and can't understand why. To control and protect herself from further abuse, she becomes overweight. She thinks, *If I'm unattractive to men, they won't hurt me.* How do we know this? Because this is exactly what one woman told us! The shame train contributes to her confusion until she realizes her addiction to food is a response to her shame.

Think about a wife who finds out her husband is addicted to pornography and has had multiple affairs. She jumps on the shame train. She questions her beauty. She moves from hurt to anger, then bitterness to depression, and then down the performance street. She becomes obsessed with her weight, body, clothes, make-up, hairstyle, and sensuality. The confusion over who she really is follows a cycle of depression and performance that's never ending. Again, a real story from a real person, riding the shame train.

....

Shame is an intense stronghold, and it leads to other strongholds that keep us imprisoned personally and relationally.

....

There are many paths where shame can take us. Shame is an intense stronghold, and it leads to other strongholds that keep us imprisoned personally and relationally. Consider how men are conditioned. "Big boys don't cry." "I control my own destiny." "If we have good sex, we must have a good marriage." "If I'm a good provider for my family, then I'm a good husband." These lies lead to empty relationships. A husband who is driven toward climbing the corporate ladder may be harsh at home. He connects only physically with his wife. The wife feels emotionally empty and doesn't respond the way he wants. He feels hurt, which leads to anger, bitterness, and depression. The husband responds by performing his way to reconnection, stonewalling, manipulation, lashing out in anger, or destruction. If none of these tactics work, he quits all together or engages in an affair that gives him a temporal good feeling.

The confusion over who he is results in his own agreements with the Enemy. Because of his unmet needs, he ends up hurting others as badly as he hurts. Destruction occurs in his relationships. His marriage deteriorates as the couple separates emotionally, causing the distance in the relationship. It's amazing how self-centered we become when we start operating with a "meet my needs or I'll punish you" mentality.

8. Read Genesis 3 and answer the following questions:

   a. How is the serpent, Satan, described (verse 1)?

b. How did he attempt to confuse Eve by his initial question (verse 1)?

c. Who did Satan contradict, causing Eve more confusion (verse 4)?

9. What did Eve *see* (meaning "convinced by") about the fruit (verse 6)? Circle as many as apply.

- It was wrong.
- It was good for food.
- It was dangerous.
- It was a protective boundary given by God.
- It was pleasing to her eyes.
- It was desirable to make her wise.

10. Once Eve and Adam sinned and realized that they were naked, what did they do (verse 7)?

11. When we find ourselves ashamed of our sin or feel a sense of shame over being sinned against, what might some of our fig leaves look like?

God helps us see how the Enemy confuses us about who we are. May His unconditional love allow us to remove the fig leaves that we've hidden behind so He can forgive and heal us.

ARE YOU ON THE SHAME TRAIN?

> Ask the Lord to open your heart and mind to His truth so that He can do His transforming work.

I (Jena) sustained multiple internal and external wounds in my car accident the summer before my senior year in high school, and they took quite some time to heal. When the accident first occurred, I was in shock. I had no idea how badly I was hurt. But after reality set in, I recognized the severity of my injuries and my need for healing and rehabilitation. I had to learn to walk all over again. I went through a long process of training and therapy. Today, all I have is a bunch of scars that tell me where I've been and never want to return.

If you've experienced shame, you may be in one of these three places:

- You're in shock. You consider the possibility that you have shame in your life, but you're unaware of the extent of your wounds. You have no idea how badly you've been wounded and how severely they're affecting your life and relationships.
- You recognize the origin of your shame and are on the road toward healing. You've begun the process of retraining yourself in truth and reembracing God's healing power over your life.
- You're walking in victory over your shame, carrying only scars from the pain you endured in your past, reminding you of where you've been and where you never intend to go again.

Wherever you are, you can be assured that
God doesn't want you to live your life in
confusion about yourself.

Wherever you are, you can be assured that God doesn't want you to live your life in confusion about yourself. He desires peace for you, not confusion. When we first shared our testimony, we would get extremely emotional as we proclaimed the gut-wrenching truths of what our lives had become. We were humbled, sometimes embarrassed, and even scared about how people would receive our painful story. The more we shared and saw God using our pain to help others, the easier it became to visit the hurt. Now we can share our scars openly. They aren't nearly as painful as the initial wounds, and God continues to use them to minister to hurting couples. That's the God we serve. He loves to take broken and marred vessels and use them to bring honor and glory to Himself. If we were perfect, unscarred vessels, we could do life apart from Him. But through our brokenness and scars, God's grace and power flow through. This way, there's no doubt that God's hand is working in and through us to bring Him glory.

When we look at the perfect example, Jesus Christ, we see two things about His scars. First, His scars are for our healing. Isaiah 53:3-5 tells us His scars save us from our sin. But secondly, in John 20:24-29, we see that Jesus shared His scars with others so they would believe. He offered comfort, courage, and hope to those who were walking in the shame of their sin. This is why the Enemy loves to keep couples wrapped up in shame. Satan knows if you find your healing in Christ and start sharing your scars with others, then the very reason Christ came will be fulfilled in your life (see 1 John 3:8).

12. Based on Isaiah 53:3-5, whose sin did He bear?

13. By bearing them, who was healed?

14. According to John 20:24-27, what was the purpose in Jesus sharing His scars with Thomas?

May we follow Jesus' example and allow His power to heal us, so we can share our scars with others and they too can be healed.

Friend, what the Enemy intends for evil, God turns to good (see Genesis 50:20). The scars in your life, whether self-inflicted or not, aren't to condemn you. They aren't present for you to feel like you have no value or are unacceptable, unapproved, or unloved. God's Word says "there is now no condemnation for those who are in Christ Jesus" (Romans 8:1). Instead, just like Christ's scars had two purposes, so do ours: to grow and strengthen us to be like Christ and to comfort others. God wants to heal us so miraculously that we have a powerful story of love to share. Following His example, we're to give others comfort, courage, and hope. In 2 Corinthians 1:3-4 we read, "Praise be to the God and Father of our Lord Jesus Christ, the Father of compassion and the God of all comfort, who comforts us in all our troubles, so that we can comfort those in any trouble with the comfort we ourselves have received from God."

Through our ministry, we meet many of God's precious children. Several years ago, we began encouraging a couple whose marriage was torn apart due to an extramarital affair. We watched the woman go through pain, anger, frustration, hatred, revenge, depression, and more. She was deteriorating physically, emotionally, and spiritually right before our eyes. But God pulled this precious girl back up and set her feet firmly on the solid rock of her Savior. She and her marriage were healed purely by the grace of God. With new understanding, she experienced the reality of Psalm 40:1-3:

I waited patiently for the LORD;
  he turned to me and heard my cry.
He lifted me out of the slimy pit,
  out of the mud and mire;
he set my feet on a rock
  and gave me a firm place to stand.
He put a new song in my mouth,
  a hymn of praise to our God.
Many will see and fear
  and put their trust in the LORD.

Two years later, this woman called us. The change in her voice was evidence that the Spirit had healed her. In our conversation, she shared the road of shame she traveled and how she spiraled to her defeat and Satan's victory. She also shared how Jesus allowed her to understand the Enemy's tactics. Miraculously, God set her free from the bondage of shame. When asked what caused the release from shame, she said she was able to help her friend walk through the same hard time in her life. She wouldn't have known how to help her friend had she not gone through it two years prior. At that moment God changed her heart and brought her to the conclusion that her suffering could be used for someone else's sake.

Do you see? God wants us to share our scars to proclaim His mercy, grace, goodness, and unfailing, never-ending, unconditional love. When we allow the Holy Spirit to change our perspective about our sin from shame to scars, He allows our scars to comfort others.

GETTING OFF THE TRAIN

While sharing our pain certainly provides healing to our shame, there is another step in the healing process. We need to cleanse ourselves from the sin that caused the shame. If it was your sin that caused your shame, you must forgive yourself and allow Christ to forgive you.

> If it was your sin that caused your
> shame, you must forgive yourself
> and allow Christ to forgive you.

Lord, we ask by Your great power that You free us from every hint of shame in our lives so we may live a life of freedom as individuals and in our marriage. Help us to do this in the strong and powerful name of Jesus, Amen.

Have you repented and accepted the forgiveness of God provided through the shed blood of His only Son, Jesus Christ? It's available to you—a free gift of grace if you will ask. It's as simple as saying, "Father God, I know I have sinned against You and You only. I know my sin separates me from fellowship with You. I recognize my need for forgiveness and accept it as a gift of grace and nothing that I've done. I change my thinking about this area of sin in my life and ask You, by the power of Your Spirit within me, to help me overcome this sin and live a life that brings You pleasure and honor. In the name of the One who makes this possible, Jesus Christ, Amen." Now you're in a partnership with God to work through, transform, and heal you from the inside out. It means removing lies and replacing them with truth, setting boundaries in your life to protect you from falling prey to the same sin, and walking so closely with God that you hear His voice telling you when to walk away from areas of temptation.

We found incredible freedom and peace with God as we took these steps toward forgiveness, repentance, and reconciliation. We've also found that some people didn't believe us. They judged and rejected us, refusing to offer us grace, love, or forgiveness. It's very painful when shame is held over someone. We also found the grace of Christ to be stronger as we simply walked with Him, trusting Him to fill in the gaps.

Are there people keeping your past sins alive, holding you captive to sins that God has already forgiven? Are there people who consider themselves judge and jury over you for the rest of your life?

Should anyone choose to judge you because of your past, they aren't questioning you, they're questioning the power of the blood of Jesus Christ to cleanse, heal, and cover sin. If anyone chooses to cast stones at your sin and shame, they are blinded by self-righteousness, not recognizing the sin in their life. This is a mockery of the shed blood of Jesus and the finished work of the Cross.

Go to God with your shame and confess your sin. Against Him and Him alone have you sinned. Accept His cleansing, covering blood, and walk away in freedom. If your sin wounded another, then you will need to go to them and ask forgiveness. (How you do that is covered in another chapter.) For now, deal with your sin against your heavenly Father and make that right. Fight for and find your freedom today by receiving His forgiveness and help.

> If the shame is from someone else's sin, give it back to them.

If the shame is from someone else's sin, give it back to them. If someone sinned against you don't take that sin as yours! It's their sin, so give it back to them and let them deal with it. So often we take other people's sin and shame upon ourselves when it wasn't ours to begin with. Release the shame to its rightful owner. This does not negate the wound or pain that was inflicted on you. You were wounded, so your healing should be your focus. That takes time and focused effort.

As you journey toward healing and freedom, you'll walk in a new dimension: the freedom of forgiveness. For you, forgiveness may not be a word you can say, much less put into practice. In time you will heal and you'll learn not only to forgive yourself, but to forgive the one who sinned against you.

Don't be locked in someone else's shame. Those who have been physically assaulted by another feel so guilty and ashamed of the incident that it eats at them like a cancer. The perpetrator may feel no remorse at all, while the victim withers.

We witnessed this firsthand when we met a couple at a conference where we had spoken. The wife looked near death. She confessed many years of marriage struggles. She also described a rape from years earlier while her husband was away in the military. Her shame was debilitating her. Her husband's shame came from guilt because he wasn't home to protect his wife. We prayed with them for God's healing and the strength to release the sin of the perpetrator by forgiving him. This was startling to them. We went home and continued to pray for this dear couple. Several weeks later, we heard from them. The wife shared that she didn't forgive the person because he deserved it, nor to exonerate him from his sin. Instead, she chose to forgive him for herself. She knew this was the only way she could be released from the shame she had carried around for so long—shame that wasn't hers to bear. Her husband had done the same. God had restored their joy, their life, and their marriage.

Are you traveling on a shame train? Are you in bondage to your sin or another's sin? Is shame keeping you from the joyous life God planned for you? There's freedom waiting for you at the foot of the cross. Lay down your shame today. Determine that sin and shame no longer have a place in your life. The blood of Jesus has covered you and Satan has no way to accuse you anymore. Declare out loud that Satan has no more place in this area of your life, that you've been forgiven and you're choosing to walk in that freedom in your life. Revelation 12:11 says, "They overcame him [Satan] by the blood of the Lamb and by the word of their testimony."

First John 1:7 says, "If we walk in the light, as he is in the light, we have fellowship with one another, and the blood of Jesus, his Son, purifies us."

15. What are we purified from?

16. How much sin?

17. Verse 9 goes on to say that if we confess our sin, God is faithful and just and will _____ our sins and _____ us from _____ unrighteousness.

18. According to Galatians 6:4, what does Paul instruct us to do?

19. In Galatians 6:5, who is responsible for their sin?

20. How are we described in 2 Corinthians 4:7?

May we be vessels of clay. Though we were once marred, we are now healed to show the all-surpassing power of our great God.

THE WEEK IN ACTION

In light of all that God has revealed to us, let's take some time with Him to look inwardly.

21. How might you describe your shame train? Is it long or short, moving slowly or quickly, full of heavy stuff or empty?

22. When you're feeling shame, do you head toward performing or destructive behavior? Why?

23. Can you pinpoint specific areas of shame in your life? If so, list them.

24. How have these played themselves out in your life and marriage?

25. Are you going through the process of forgiveness for your own sin? Are you letting go of sin that isn't yours? If yes, describe your journey. If no, what is holding you back?

Higher-Risk Option: This whole chapter may have been high-risk. It is the most risky chapter of all. You may be emotionally exhausted. If so, know that your Father is proud of you and wants you to simply rest in Him for a little while and let Him love on you. You have made it through, and though tough, you're at the place where you'd like to share what God has revealed with your spouse. If so, we encourage you to share with him/her all that God has done in your life that will bring freedom to areas of your marriage.

We also recognize you may have been convicted of a shameful sin against your spouse that you feel led to confess. Based upon the severity of shame that you are willing to disclose, there are a few cautions we'd like to address:

- Make sure you've prayed and asked the Lord to prepare your heart and your spouse's heart. Pray, too, that He will present the perfect time for you to share.
- Make sure you and your spouse are at a place relationally to have this discussion. Have you practiced the previous chapters of this book together? Are you safe with one another? Are you walking with God in such a way that He is supplying your needs? Have you worked through the Enemy's lies and your family upbringing and discussed how they have affected your marriage? Have you made peace with God over these areas of sin in your life?
- Consider having a Christian mediator help you walk through any serious issue.
- Listen and be obedient to what the Lord is prompting you to do.

Let God take you on a journey to reveal the shame that has held you and your marriage hostage. Let God heal you so you can walk in freedom and then share your scars to comfort and encourage others on similar journeys. Set yourself free from the prison where sin has held you shackled for so long. Embrace the forgiveness of God. Tell others there is hope. It's the most freeing thing you will ever do.

THE SHAME TRAIN

John 11:4,17-40—The Story of Lazarus

_____ people, shame _____.

Shame is a result of _____.

Hurt leads to _____.

The Road of Anger:

_____

_____

_____

_____

_____

Anger is all about_____.

Anger can cause us to become a:

_____   _____   _____

(Mary)   (Martha)   (Jesus)

Ask the Holy Spirit to help you _____,
_____, and _____.

Solvers _____

_____.

Now turn to appendix A (page 177) and record your resolution.

Chapter Six

OWN YOUR STUFF

As iron sharpens iron, so one man sharpens another.

Proverbs 27:17

It's been our sincere prayer that you and your marriage have experienced newfound freedom, purpose, and passion as you get real with the Lord and with each other. We hope you see the deliberateness of this journey. We pray you've removed some masks as you've learned how to hold each other's hearts well, find your needs fulfilled in Christ, and fight the Enemy while being delivered from strongholds and shame. This week is a critical week. It's easy to stop about halfway through a study, but don't. There's more the Lord wants to do in your life and your marriage. As you turn the corner and head down the back stretch, we believe the Lord is going to faithfully complete the good work He started (see Philippians 1:6).

This is also a critical week, because everyone faces conflict. It happens in our marriages, in the lives of our kids, at work, with neighbors, and in small groups and churches. Yes, conflict is inevitable. How many conflicts can you identify in your life right now?

1. List a couple of the conflicts in your marriage right now.

Read Proverbs 27:17, and ask yourself this question: What is God after in the midst of conflict? Until we learn to look at our conflicts the way Christ looks at them, we're going to make a mess of our relationships. In fact, we should ask this question about everything we face in life. There is so much freedom, purpose, and transformation when we're able to see everything that happens in our lives as divine opportunities for Christ to sharpen us into His image. That's exactly why we must learn to handle conflict with a Christlike view in a Christlike manner.

....

Until we learn to look at our conflicts the way Christ looks at them, we're going to make a mess of our relationships.

....

CHOICES IN THE MIDST OF CONFLICT

Have you noticed the innumerable choices we're offered? Count the books at your bookstore, tally the options at your favorite restaurant, notice the myriad of selections at the department store. From ice-cream flavors to fashions, our world is filled with choices. Conflict is no different. It, too, comes with a set of choices. We've identified three we believe couples choose. As you read, consider which one you most often make.

Choosing to Retreat and Avoid

The first choice we have in conflict is to retreat. Many of us simply don't like conflict! We'll do whatever it takes to avoid it. We quickly withdraw, shut down, and isolate ourselves. When feelings are raw, you're feeling wounded, and emotions are high, it's easy to retreat. Yes, sometimes retreating is a good choice (briefly), as long as you set a time to work through the conflict. Sometimes you need a cooling-off period. It's better to walk away and let things settle than to continue the conflict in an ungodly and unholy way. No one has to apologize for an unkind word left unspoken. Cooling off, being a person of self-control, being considerate of your spouse's feelings, and knowing your relational weak points so you don't wound each other are all good things.

But there's also unhealthy retreat. This is the person who continually retreats—who disengages in the relationship and avoids conflict at all cost. Continual retreaters never resolve their conflicts. Most often, they refuse to look at themselves, to stay engaged in the relationship, or allow Christ to use it as a moment of transformation and refining. Over time the continual retreater turns into a stuffer. Years of stuffing hurt and frustration turns into bitterness. The unresolved conflict and bitterness then turns into anger (remember last week). Much like a shaken can of soda, one incident, whether small or large, can pop the cap of their heart. They find themselves spewing angry words like daggers in all directions, doing serious damage.

2. Jonah was a retreater. God told him to go to Nineveh and to speak on His behalf (see Jonah 1:2). Instead, because of fear, Jonah ran to Tarshish. Take a moment and turn back to the listening guide for week 4 ("A Look at Our Legacy") and write the remedy for fear.

3. As we learned, fear can be an enormous motivator. Circle the fear-based reasons that motivate you to choose to retreat and avoid conflict.

- Fear of being hurt
- Fear of being confronted
- Fear of failure
- Fear of having to change
- Fear of being wrong
- Fear of being caught

Perhaps, instead of retreating in fear, the most loving thing you could do is to push through your fear and activate your love. Remember, the perfect love of Christ will cast out all our fear.

4. Read 1 John 4:18, and write a prayer to Christ. Tell Him what you're afraid of. Ask Him to fill you with His perfect love.

5. Ask God to help you answer this question about your conflicts: *Lord, in the midst of this conflict, how should I love my spouse?* Write what you hear the Lord saying.

CHOOSING TO REBEL

The second choice in conflict is to rebel. If you're not one who retreats, you might be one who continually rebels. Rebellion means what you think it does: defiant, stubborn, obstinate, stiff-necked, and disobedient. Continual rebellers always have to be right, always have to have the last word, and rarely admit they're wrong. Consequently, they have a hard time owning their stuff. They're like Arthur Fonzarelli, aka The Fonz, from the TV show *Happy Days*: They just can't say they are wrrrrr . . . wrong!

Why do we feel the need to dig in our heels and come out fighting? Certainly, Isaiah 53:6 says we each want our own way. The world we live in with its Burger King, "have it your way" mentality certainly promotes this. Ephesians 4:22 and James 4:1-2 remind us there's a battle waging in our souls, because we have insatiable desires. Simply put, we'll do whatever is needed to get our own way. Just like continual retreaters, continual rebellers don't want to admit they're wrong. They come out fighting, deflecting, and blaming others for their behavior. The rebellious person never has conviction or sees the need for change so the conflict and pain continue in the relationship. They remain the same in their ungodly behavior because they've passed the blame to others by rationalizing and justifying their actions.

> Our problem isn't that we don't know what to do, but our unwillingness to do it!

Within all of us is a rebellious nature that wants our own way. That's why we're convinced of this one truth: Our problem isn't that we don't know what to do, but our unwillingness to do it! Too many times, especially in the midst of conflict, we choose the selfish choice rather than the selfless one. The Word of God speaks about the heart condition and the consequences of rebellion. Read the following passages and ask the Lord to reveal to you where you might struggle with rebellion.

6. According to Isaiah 53:6, where has each of us turned?

7. Read James 4:17. What does the Word of God call rebellion against doing good?

8. Read Proverbs 29:1. What is the result of continual rebellion?

9. What are rebellious people unwilling to do according to Isaiah 30:9?

10. In light of God's Word, how do you think the warnings in these passages of Scripture could help you in the midst of conflict?

We understand how hard this is in the midst of conflict. But in the midst of conflict, when emotions and feelings are raw, if you choose your own sinful way and rebel, you'll have a hard time listening to your spouse. When you rebel, destruction of the relationship is inevitable. How easy it is for this to happen. We remember so many arguments where we walked down this very path. Our conflicts were full of pride, selfishness, and stubbornness, driving us to the point of being deaf to one another. Just as it's so easy to retreat, it's so easy to rebel. That's why we said earlier, we must learn to handle conflict with a Christlike view in a Christlike manner. Remember, God is calling us to live at a higher place, rising above our fleshly tendencies that so strongly drive us.

CHOOSING RESPONSIBILITY — OWNING YOUR STUFF

Often, there's one continual retreater and one continual rebeller in a marriage. It's hard to see conflict as an iron-sharpening-iron opportunity for transformation and growth, but it is. The retreater and rebeller need each other. That's why the right choice, the biblical choice, is to see conflict as an opportunity to grow in the image of Christ by laying aside selfishness, fear, and pride while owning your stuff. Choosing to take responsibility for your actions in the midst of conflict always results in a more genuine, grace-filled relationship.

Here's how we learned this. Like so many of you, we learn so much about ourselves by watching our kids. Our daughter Jorja was four years old, sitting on the floor watching television. Cole, our seven-year-old son, entered the room and, with total disregard for Jorja, changed the channel. Cole constantly picked at Jorja because he thought that's what big brothers did, or at least could get away with. He'd also been warned by both of us that one day Jorja would grow up and repay him, and we were going to let her.

That day came as we heard a blood-curdling scream from our den. Jorja had grabbed Cole by the hair in a full-on death grip. She was pulling it so tightly that he was screaming at the top of his lungs. The moment she saw us, her face went from a teeth-gritting growl to a full-fledged grin! Jena escorted Cole and Jorja to the sofa to discuss what happened. Cole's response to what he did was, "She pulled my hair!" Jena said, "Cole, I didn't ask you what Jorja did; I asked you what you did!" He said, "Big boys don't watch kiddie shows, so I changed the channel." When Jorja was asked about the part she played in the conflict, her answer was much the same: "Cole changed the channel!"

Doesn't that sound just like some married couple, entrenched in a conflict? We're just little kids in big people bodies! Blaming, shaming, and passing the buck, blinded and refusing to own our stuff while trying to get the speck out of our brother's eye (see Matthew 7:3). Way too many couples are blaming the other for their behavior, rarely admitting their part in the conflict.

Jena then talked with Cole and Jorja about their choices, selfishness, wanting their own way, and ultimately their sin. She asked Cole and Jorja to do a few things. She asked them to confess their sin, call it sin, and seek the other's forgiveness. Jorja was required to say, "Cole, I pulled your hair and it was wrong. It was sin. I am sorry. Will you forgive me?" And Cole had to do the same. As soon as we sent them off, the Spirit of God convicted us both. We were reminded that we just asked our kids to do something we rarely do! Wow, talk about conviction. If you're going to bring wholeness to your marriage, you're going to have to start owning your stuff. Oh, what our marriages, homes, churches, communities, and world would look like if we would just stop rationalizing our choices, retreating and rebelling in our actions, and call sin what it really is. If couples could just let this principle melt into their hearts, we believe their marital conflicts would dramatically change.

> If you're going to bring wholeness to your marriage, you're going to have to start owning your stuff.

11. As you think back on conflicts in your marriage, we want to challenge you to do what we asked our kids to do: simply take responsibility to own your stuff. Before we show you what it takes to own your stuff, ask the Lord to search your heart. What conflicts do you have in your marriage? What stuff do you need to own?

12. Read Psalm 4:4 and 139:23-24. Be silent before the Lord and ask Him to fulfill this Scripture. Write down your requests and desires:

"Know my heart." Lord, my heart is . . .

"Know my anxious thoughts." Lord, my thoughts are anxious because . . .

"See within me." Lord, show how my choices have been offensive to You and to my spouse . . .

"Lead me." Lord, lead me in the midst of this conflict by . . .

WHAT IT TAKES TO OWN YOUR STUFF

After we were remarried, it took months of evaluating to discover what happened to cause the breakdown of our marriage. Much of what we're sharing in this study is the result of our journey toward authenticity and wholeness. If anyone ever made wrong choices in the midst of conflict, we were definitely that couple. During the first eight years of our first marriage, we had way too much retreating and rebelling and very little owning of our stuff. During the last half of this chapter, we want to invite you to walk the pathway we walked to find what it takes to own your stuff. We've been told, "If you have the Word of God, then you have an answer; if you don't, then all you have is an opinion." So this last part of the chapter is going to be digging into the Word of God. We want you to get into Scripture and find the truth for your life. We're going to look at three things that are critical to owning your stuff and handling conflict well. They're God's destiny for you, God's desire for you, and God's design for you.

GOD'S DESTINY FOR YOU

As we've already stated, until we learn to look at our conflicts the way Christ looks at our conflicts, we're going to make a mess of our relationships. To really understand this statement, you need to fully understand God's destiny for your life—to look at your life the way Christ looks at it.

13. Read Ephesians 1:4; 4:24; 2 Corinthians 7:1; and 1 Peter 1:13-16.

a. What is God's chosen destiny for your life?

b. When you think of holiness as God's destiny for you, what thoughts come to mind?

Misconceptions of holiness keep us from living the abundant, passion-filled, purpose-driven life of a Christian. Too many Christians have boiled their faith down to a "God is good, you are bad, now stop it" approach. God has so much more in store for you than just managing your sin. He has an abundant, exciting, joy-filled faith walk prepared for you with His end destiny being holiness.

Do you believe God knows what's best for you? If so, then think about this: To be holy simply means to be set apart unto God. In other words, you're totally sold out to God. You're an ambassador of His mission. You're available for His awesome and special purpose. To be sure, holiness is more about your character than your behavior. It's the very nature of God being reproduced in your heart. Holiness is what emanates from God. It's His essence. And because it's His essence, it should be ours. Holiness is a process and daily journey of striving to be more like Christ.

14. Read the following Scriptures and match them to the corresponding truth.

1 Peter 1:15	Do it all in Christ's name
2 Corinthians 4:16	Be holy in all you do
John 17:17	Renewed inwardly daily
Acts 17:28	Set apart by truth
Colossians 3:17	In Him I live
Ephesians 5:1	Imitate Christ

These Scriptures, and the entire Word of God for that matter, show us what to do. What if they became the foundation you built on in the midst of conflict? What if you embraced the fact that Christ died so that you could be holy? Would your choices and character look different if they were based on the truth that "in Him you live and move and have your being" (see Acts 17:28)? What would your marriage look like if you simply renewed yourself inwardly day by day as you went through life? What would change if you really did everything in Christ's name because you strived to be holy in all that you do, being set apart by truth? Would your conflict look different if you imitated Christ in the midst of it? We believe all of this, because our experience has proved it! Perhaps you (as we used to) have a difficult time seeing Christ in the crisis because you've simply lost your pursuit of holiness. Do you want a radical, biblical approach to owning your stuff? Then pursue holiness in the midst of the conflict. After all, Hebrews 12:14 reminds us "without holiness no one will see the Lord."

GOD'S DESIRE FOR YOU

God's destiny for you is holiness because He has an incredible desire for you. What's this desire? Intimacy! Let this sink in. Intimacy! The Creator of the universe, our holy, righteous, and loving heavenly Father, desires intimacy with *you*. James MacDonald, in his book *Gripped by the Greatness of God*, writes:

> *God displays holiness as the central and defining essence of his character. I know some people think God is defined by love, but I would beg to differ. If love was at the very center of God's nature, then He could have welcomed us into heaven without the atoning death of His Son, Jesus. Fact is, God's holiness demanded that sin be paid for, and then His love compelled Him to pay the price Himself.*[1]

Do you see this? Because of God's holiness, His love compelled Him to die for us, so we could be redeemed and restored (see 1 Peter 1:18-23). God desires a face-to-face, intimate relationship with us. Christ even prayed this prayer for you.

15. Read John 17:20-23 and fill in this blank: "I have given them the glory that you gave me, that they may be _____ _____:"

16. Did you notice the colon at the end of verse 22? Christ is defining His desire. Complete this sentence: "I in _____ and you in _____!"

Christ is praying that we'd be as intimate with Him as He is with His Father. Once we have intimacy with Christ, we can experience intimacy with one another. Here's the bottom line: Without the pursuit of holiness and embracing God's desire for intimacy, we won't experience the abundant life our heavenly Father so painfully provided.

We also believe Christ prayed this powerful prayer for you because He knows that intimacy with Christ creates intimacy in your marriage. Intimacy is simply this: into me, I will let you see. It's about letting Christ into every area of your life. It's about transparency, no more masks, no more games, no more hiding. Intimacy in marriage is the same thing. It's about openness, transparency, and oneness (see Genesis 2:24; John 17:22). Intimacy opposes choosing to retreat or rebel. Make no mistake about it, there's a direct relationship between our intimate relationship with Christ and our intimate relationship with one another. That's why holiness is God's destiny and intimacy is His desire.

> Intimacy opposes choosing
> to retreat or rebel.

GOD'S DESIGN FOR YOU

Years ago, we went on a quest for finding our identity in Christ. What we found was a new freedom and power for our Christian walk. God's design, who He says we are, was incredibly liberating. No longer were we going to be the rule-keeping, performance-based Christian couple. You see, rule-keeping, performance-based couples are only as good as their latest performance. As long as they perform well or don't break the rules they are good. But the moment they mess up (and they will), everything changes. Years of rule keeping and performance causes a fragile marriage.

17. A couple usually swings from one extreme of perform, perform, perform for approval to the other extreme of just quitting all together.

This is why men and women say, "I try and I try and I try and it's
_____" (fill in
the blank).

But when a man and a woman discover who Christ says they are
and they begin living in that design, their lives and marriage change.
Jena's Bible study *Authentic Woman: In Search of the Genuine Article*
was written just for women to help them find this out. We won't have
an identity problem when we see ourselves the way God sees us.

So let's turn to the Word of God and find God's design for you.

18. Read these Scriptures and write who God says you are.

Genesis 1:27

John 15:15

Romans 8:29

Romans 8:37

Galatians 4:6-7

Ephesians 1:4

Ephesians 2:10

Ephesians 4:23-24

Colossians 2:9-10

These Scriptures are by no means exhaustive. The Word of God is full of Scriptures about who God says you are. How comforting to be reminded that you were made in His image and predestined to be conformed to the likeness of Christ. The very God of the universe calls you His friend and a conqueror! Not only are you a friend but a son and an heir. Christ died so that you would be holy and blameless in His sight, created to do good works which He prepared in advance for you. The more you walk in this identity, the more you change your attitude about who you are. You're compelled to exchange your old ways for new ones because you were created to be like God in true righteousness and holiness. For in Christ, all the fullness of the divine nature exists, and you have been given fullness in Christ.

19. If God's destiny is holiness, His desire is intimacy—and this is your identity! What are you to do in response? Read these passages and write your answers.

Romans 8:12-17

2 Corinthians 5:14-17

Galatians 5:16-26

1 Peter 1:13-16

1 Peter 2:16-17

....

When we don't pursue holiness in our conflicts, we simply won't see Christ in our homes.

....

In the midst of conflict, it's definitely a challenge to own your stuff. It's much easier to retreat or rebel. But God has a bigger plan. We hope you see that now. Yes, even in the midst of conflict and especially through conflict, God wants to perfect you. He wants you to handle conflict differently. He wants you to be set apart in your thinking, feeling, and acting because His destiny for you is holiness. When we don't pursue holiness in our conflicts, we simply won't see Christ in our homes. Remember, our selfish desires and wanting our own way is at the root of all our relationship discord. Selfishness destroys marriages. But praise God for His amazing plan.

His plan for everyone on this earth is to trust Him with their life. From the moment of our salvation, God works on recreating Himself in us. He is after the creation of true holiness and true righteousness in your life. He wants you to partner with the Holy Spirit, allowing Him to do the deep work of ridding you of anything that contaminates or corrupts His presence in your life.

We believe that God does His deepest transforming work in the marriage relationship. We also believe God does His deepest work in the midst of trials, stress, struggles, and conflicts. No wonder marriage is so hard. No wonder conflict in marriage is so critical. No wonder we need to see our conflicts the way Christ sees them. After all, He is after so much more than just the fixing of our problems, He's after the formation of His character in our souls (see Galatians 4:19).

THE WEEK IN ACTION

We hope you see the power in this chapter. To make it come alive, let's make it personal.

20. Which choice do you usually make in the midst of conflict? Circle one.

- Retreat and Avoid
- Rebel
- Own Your Stuff

21. Why do you think you normally make this choice?

22. We talked a lot about holiness. Holiness is more about character than behavior. On the lines below, mark where you are currently in regard to your walk with Christ and your pursuit of holiness.

Religiously Active   Spiritually Intimate

Sin Management/Rule Keeping   Daily Walking with Christ

23. What's one thing you can do right now to pursue holiness?

Higher-Risk Option: At the beginning of the chapter you wrote down some one-word descriptions of current or recent conflicts in your marriage. Considering that holiness is God's destiny for you and your marriage, and knowing that intimacy with you is His desire while you find your identity in the Word of God, answer this question:

24. How can you own your stuff and demonstrate Christ in the midst of conflict?

Most of us mishandle the conflicts in our lives. Chances are you're in the midst of a conflict right now. Write a prayer below, asking the Lord to forgive you for how you have mishandled it or for revelation about how to handle it. We know this is risky stuff. We know relationships are hard. We also know the Word of God works. Based on the severity of your circumstance, you might need to take someone with you. You might need to involve a counselor or pastor, but we encourage you to go to your spouse with all humility, own your stuff, and work it out. Remember Hebrews 12:14: "Make every effort to live in peace with all men and to be holy; without holiness no one will see the Lord."

25. Write your own prayer here.

OWN YOUR STUFF

Luke 18:9-14—The Pharisee and The Tax Collector

The Jews defined relationship by their _____.

Jesus defined relationship by your _____.

With God, we exchange _____

for _____.

In marriage, we exchange _____

for _____.

Pharisee	Tax Collector
Considered more spiritual	Considered less spiritual
Stood up	Stood at a distance
Prayed about himself	Asked for mercy
Owned nothing	Owned it all
Proud	Humble

Are you a marital Pharisee?

Intimate relationships hinge on _____.

Humility is _____ (John 15:5).

Humility is _____ (Matthew 7:1-5).

Now turn to appendix A (page 177) and record your resolution.

Chapter Seven

LET IT GO

Father, forgive them, for they do not know what they are doing.

Luke 23:34

As we learned last week, mishandled conflict causes a lot of damage. You may still be suffering the consequences of conflict that wasn't handled in a godly manner. Don't despair; there's hope. It's called forgiveness. So, let's turn our focus now on letting it go through applying authentic forgiveness in our marriages.

Even though we both discovered a relationship with Christ at an early age, it wasn't until we experienced our divorce and remarriage that we understood how deeply we'd been forgiven through Christ. If you've never accepted the forgiveness of Christ, then you'll never be able to truly forgive others. Your first step toward letting it go and finding true, authentic forgiveness must start with accepting the grace of God. If you've never accepted Christ as your Lord and Savior, settle the issue right now by talking with Him openly and honestly. Turn to the appendix for help with this life-changing decision.

WHAT FORGIVENESS IS NOT

Before we look at what authentic forgiveness demands, let's look at some common misconceptions about forgiveness. First of all, forgiveness is not forgetting! We've talked with countless couples who thought they must both forgive and forget. Yes, Scripture clearly says in Isaiah 43:25, "I, even I, am he who blots out your transgressions, for my own sake, and remembers your sins no more."

> Forgiveness is not forgetting. You must choose what to do with the memory.

God, through His sovereign grace, forgives us our transgressions and remembers them no more. However, we're finite-minded people, not infinite God. We also have an enemy who accuses us day and night (see Revelation 12:10). No wonder when conflict arises, the first thing your enemy does is remind you of the past. Frustrated, you figure you'll never get through all your stuff because the memory is still there. Because you can't forget, you begin to doubt whether you've really given or received forgiveness. As people with limitations, we don't have the ability to forget. But we can choose how we'll respond when confronted with memories of a past hurt or sin. This is why authentic forgiveness is not forgetting. You must choose what to do with the memory. You must refuse to allow the Enemy to keep you hostage to the things you can't forget.

> *Finally, brothers, whatever is true, whatever is noble, whatever is right, whatever is pure, whatever is lovely, whatever is admirable—if anything is excellent or praiseworthy—think about such things. Whatever you have learned or received or heard from me, or seen in me—put it into practice. And the God of peace will be with you. (Philippians 4:8-9)*

When we think on these things, the God of peace is with us. He replaces painful memories with His love and grace. This provides great strength as you demonstrate forgiveness to those who need it. Truly, God can transform your mind as you fill it with the truths of His Word.

Forgiveness isn't automatic reconciliation.

Second, forgiveness isn't automatic reconciliation. We've been taught that after we say, "I'm sorry," everything is fine. But it's not that simple. Forgiveness happens first, reconciliation follows. In order for reconciliation to follow, change needs to happen in the lives of those in conflict. This ultimately happens as each person recognizes and repents of their sin. Acts 26:20 offers a biblical definition of repentance and reconciliation: "repent and turn to God and prove their repentance by their deeds." Working through conflict in a God-honoring way can transform us for the better. This transformation takes time and a partnership with the Holy Spirit. This is why forgiveness is not automatic reconciliation. It takes only one person to forgive, but it takes two to reconcile. It takes time to rebuild trust and move beyond the hurt. This happens as you prove your repentance by your deeds. If you're truly repentant, your actions will underscore your words (see 2 Corinthians 7:10). Make no mistake, God desires for you to forgive others, to reconcile and move forward in freedom with Christ. Our God is a God of reconciliation. This is why He sent Jesus—to reconcile a lost and dying world. Jesus offers the gift of forgiveness to all who will receive. Once you receive His gift, you can forgive others and then begin the journey of reconciliation.

Forgiveness is not for the other person.

Lastly, forgiveness isn't for the other person, it's for you. Remember again Isaiah 43:25. God says, "I . . . am he who blots out your transgressions, for my own sake." God forgave us for His own sake. It was a measure of His love because He wanted so desperately to be in relationship with us. You and I stand forgiven today because of who God is, not who we are. In the same way, when we forgive a spouse who hurt us, we forgive them for who God is, not who they are. In other words, you don't forgive others because they are worthy, you forgive others because Christ is worthy. This is why forgiveness isn't for the other person, it's for you. You may never hear the words "I'm sorry" from your spouse. But even if you don't you are still commanded to forgive. Withholding forgiveness, then, is a sin. This disobedience causes our unforgiving heart great anxiety, bitterness, depression, and hatred. It's a deadly cancer, eating at your soul.

We speak at marriage conferences across the country. Once, an obviously burdened woman came to us. She said things had to drastically change over the next twenty-four hours or she was divorcing her husband. Years of pain had taken its toll on her and her health. She looked at us and asked, "Are you telling me I have to forgive my husband for everything he's done wrong?" Jena tenderly said, "Yes, dear lady, you do. You may never hear the words 'I'm sorry.' You may never hear the words 'Will you forgive me?' You didn't deserve this, yet you must still forgive." As we concluded, the woman's husband joined us. We witnessed the incredible forgiving power of God. Her husband confessed to his sin. As they sat in the pew and cried, God began mending two hearts. A marriage was restored because one person understood she must forgive for herself and not her husband.

1. Circle any of the three misconceptions of forgiveness you've struggled with.

- Forgiving and forgetting
- Forgiving and reconciling
- Forgiving for others

2. According to 2 Corinthians 10:4-5, what do we destroy and how?

3. When Scripture says to take your thoughts captive, it means to bring those thoughts under the authority of Christ. What thoughts do you need to bring under the authority of Christ?

4. How can Philippians 4:4-9 help you with this?

5. Remember the battle is played in the battlefield of the mind. How does this live out in the three misconceptions of forgiveness?

AUTHENTIC FORGIVENESS—LETTING IT GO

If forgiveness is not forgetting, not automatic reconciliation, and not for the other person but for you, then what is authentic forgiveness? How do you get there? It starts with the awareness that every one of us stands in need of forgiveness. So often we look at others instead of ourselves. It's so easy to see others' faults and sins. Marriages will change when we focus on our own faults instead of our spouse's. This is why the Word of God commands us to do self-reflection (see Matthew 7:3; 2 Corinthians 13:5; Galatians 6:1). It's here we see the depravity of our souls. When we confess our sin before a Holy God, authentic forgiveness begins. Have you heard someone say, "If I hurt your feelings, I'm sorry"? This is a lack of owning your stuff apology. We're not talking about glazing things over or minimizing the behavior with an "if I" apology. No, authentic forgiveness includes authentic confession.

The Greek word for confess is *homologeo*, which means "to declare, acknowledge or profess."[1] Confessing our sins is professing and agreeing with God about our sinful behavior. It's the first step toward forgiveness. We must do this first with God and then with those we've sinned against (see James 5:16).

> Marriages will change when couples
> take their eyes off of their spouse
> and focus on themselves instead.

How do you differentiate between a blanket apology and authentic forgiveness? This is difficult for couples when trust is low and pain is real. The Word of God reminds us we can't judge another's motives. We must also be careful how we judge others because we'll be judged likewise. There are, however, some indicators of authentic forgiveness. Again, true confession is always partnered with repentance. Repentance means to have a change of mind which results in a change in the direction of your will. You recognize you're in the wrong place, headed in the wrong direction. You agree with God about your choices that resulted in your sin. This is the story of the prodigal son in Luke 15. Verse 17 says, "When he came to his senses." Verse 18 says, "I will set out and go back to my father and say to him: Father, I have sinned against heaven and against you." True confession and repentance always involve returning to our heavenly Father, as well as to the person we sinned against. Did you see it? "I have sinned against heaven and you."

True confession and repentance also result in a changed life. Countless couples have told us, "Their words mean nothing to me. I've heard it all before, but things stay the same." Could it be because there was no true repentance? In other words, there is more worldly sorrow than godly sorrow. Second Corinthians 7:10 reminds us, "Godly sorrow brings repentance that leads to salvation and leaves no regret, but worldly sorrow brings death." Godly sorrow causes change in a person's life. Godly sorrow means you see your sin the way God sees it. It causes grief, mourning, and heaviness of your heart until it is dealt with, repented of, and forgiven. In Psalm 51:17 David writes, "The sacrifices of God are a broken spirit; a broken and contrite heart." The word *contrite* literally means to be crushed like powder. This is powerful because when our spirits are hard-hearted and unwilling to agree with God, sin and suffering continue. When our spirits are broken, becoming crushed like powder, the Holy Spirit blows in and washes away our sin.

Worldly sorrow is simply, "I'm sorry I got caught." Worldly sorrow involves self-justification and excuse making. It's the opposite of godly sorrow because it doesn't involve confession, repentance, and transformation. Choosing worldly sorrow over godly sorrow results in a vicious cycle of inauthentic forgiveness as the same issues repeatedly crop up.

For true forgiveness to occur, we must ask for the cleansing power of God in our lives. We must ask God to help us see ourselves and our sinfulness so we truly experience godly sorrow. Then as the psalmist begged in Psalm 51:10, we pray, "Create in me a pure heart, O God, and renew a steadfast spirit within me."

6. On the line below, mark where your marriage relationship currently is:

|---|

Same Issues Repeatedly   We're Making Progress

7. Do you most often find yourself operating with godly sorrow or worldly sorrow? What changes do you think you should make?

8. Read Psalm 51:10-12 and reword David's prayer as your own.

THE CHOICES OF AN AUTHENTIC FORGIVER

With confession, repentance, and godly sorrow as our backdrop, let's look at three critical choices an authentic forgiver must make: to forgive as Christ forgives, to leave the past in the past, and to take the initiative to forgive. But before we do, let's look at the Hebrew word for *forgive*, which is *aphiemi*. It means "to send away or depart." It also means to accept the consequences of the other person's action and not hold it against them.

As we studied the meaning of the word *aphiemi*, we found it odd that the *Strong's Exhaustive Concordance* referenced "of a husband divorcing his wife."[2] This didn't sound like forgiveness to us. But as we thought it through, we realized this is exactly what happens in a divorce. You bid your spouse to go away—depart from you—and end the relationship. You're no longer bound to them emotionally or physically. This is what we should do with sin! We should depart from it and no longer be bound to it. We should disregard it and flee from it, avoiding every appearance of evil (see 1 Thessalonians 5:22; 2 Timothy 2:22). Instead of divorcing from each other, what if a couple decided to divorce themselves from the sin that resided in their relationship? What would happen to their marriage?

Instead of divorcing from each other, what
if a couple decided to divorce themselves
from the sin that resided in their
relationship?

FORGIVE AS CHRIST FORGIVES

The first choice of an authentic forgiver is to forgive as Christ forgives. In Matthew 6:12-15, Jesus teaches us to pray this way:

> *Forgive us our debts, as we also have forgiven our debtors. And lead us not into temptation, but deliver us from the evil one. For if you forgive men when they sin against you, your heavenly Father will also forgive you. But if you do not forgive men their sins, your Father will not forgive your sins.*

There's no room for misunderstanding here. Verse 14 makes a definitive statement of what happens when you don't forgive. You can't accept Christ's forgiveness and not be willing to offer it to those who have sinned against you. Christ was sinless, yet He was sinned against (see 1 Peter 2:22-25). As Jesus hung on the cross He said, "Father, forgive them, for they do not know what they are doing" (Luke 23:34). Aren't you thankful for God's forgiveness, which has set you free from the penalties of sin? Sadly, it's easy to forget what was paid for our forgiveness.

In Romans 6:1-7, Paul addresses the relationship between sin, forgiveness, and grace. He asks whether grace abounds so sin can abound more. His answer is absolutely not. The measure of grace and forgiveness you offer others will be the same measure you'll receive. We all need reminding of the forgiveness we so freely accept and so quickly forget. It's through this remembrance that we return to God's grace and then extend it to others. As we understand the depth of love and forgiveness we've been given, we're compelled to love and forgive as Christ (see Luke 7:47-50). We must divorce the sin and hold onto it no longer.

> As we understand the depth of love and forgiveness we've been given, we're compelled to love and forgive as Christ.

9. Write a prayer of thanksgiving to the Lord for His forgiveness and the freedom you have because of it.

10. Praise God that you stand forgiven. Now choose to forgive as Christ forgives. Read Galatians 5:13-17 and then connect these words.

Called to be	You will be destroyed
Freedom but no	You will not gratify your sinful nature
If you bite and devour	Indulgence in sinful nature
Live by the Spirit	Free

11. Read 1 Peter 2:16 and fill in the blank. Don't use your freedom as a
_____ for evil.

12. How does this apply to you, and how you should forgive others?

Leave the Past in the Past

The second choice of authentic forgiveness is to leave the past in the past. This choice requires great discipline and self-control. Dale's mom calls it the "bury the hatchet" principle. Some people bury the hatchet with the handle down and others with the handle up. Those who bury it with the handle up can easily pick up the hatchet when the next conflict arises. They use the past as a weapon. First Corinthians 13 reminds us that love doesn't keep a record of wrong. It doesn't exhume past sin once it's been forgiven. Aren't you glad that Christ doesn't remember your sins? Aren't you glad He leaves the past in the past? His forgiveness is genuine because He doesn't keep a record of wrong (see Isaiah 43:25).

Making this choice is hard. The battle rages between our Spirit-led faith and our emotionally driven feelings. That's why authentic forgivers decide what they're going to do before they enter a battle. After we confessed our wrongs to one another during our knee-to-knee session, we were forgiving and forgiven. Three short weeks later, the Enemy attacked my (Jena's) thoughts by reminding me of all the cruel things that had been said during the trial. One night when Dale returned from work I greeted him with, "I can't believe you let those people get on a witness stand and say all those hateful things about me! How could you do that?" Dale replied, "Jena, I thought you forgave me for that!" Bringing up the offense didn't mean that authentic forgiveness hadn't occurred back in the counseling session. It did mean I made the wrong choice that day. We all respond in wrong ways and are faced once again with the need to forgive and be forgiven. When a sin has been forgiven, you still wage a war with your mind about whether to dwell on it or bring it up again.

We learn how to wage war in 2 Corinthians 10:3-6:

> *For though we live in the world, we do not wage war as the world does. The weapons we fight with are not the weapons of the world. On the contrary, they have divine power to demolish strongholds. We demolish arguments and every pretension that sets itself up against the knowledge of God, and we take captive every thought to make it obedient to Christ. And we will be ready to punish every act of disobedience, once your obedience is complete.*

....

When you're tempted to dwell on the past, remember your spouse is not your enemy.

....

What does this mean? First it means you have to recognize the source of the battle. If you don't know where the war is fought and who the war is against, you won't know what weapons to use. When you're tempted to dwell on the past, remember your spouse is not your enemy. Remembering the past and returning to a conflict is a spiritual issue. It's either God resurfacing an area in your life to continue His work of holiness in your marriage or it's the Enemy in his relentless pursuit of destruction (see Ephesians 6:12). We must take our thoughts captive under the obedience of Christ. Remember, it's intimacy with our heavenly Father that allows us to wield the right weapons. When you're attacked by rising pressure and the Enemy piles on accusations, you'll be able to fight against any stronghold, argument, or pretense. If you have more of Jesus in your life and less of you, it'll be easier to choose to leave the past in the past.

When we learned to authentically forgive, we made a covenant to never speak of past sins committed against one another, except for the edification and building up of others (see Hebrews 3:13; 1 Thessalonians 5:11). We made a covenant to only use our journey to help others facing similar struggles. That's why we wrote this book. We want God to use our experiences to provide help and hope for you (see 2 Corinthians 1:3-4).

13. How hard is it for you to leave the past in the past? Mark where you are on the line.

|———————————————————————————————————|

Fairly Easy   Extremely Hard

14. What conflict(s) keeps returning to you?

15. Is God doing a work in your life or is the Enemy the cause?

16. What do you think should be your response?

17. What is one way you can take your thoughts captive? (Read these Scriptures for guidance: Psalm 48:9; 119:59; Romans 12:3; Philippians 3:7-14; 4:8.)

TAKE INITIATIVE TO FORGIVE

Authentic forgivers not only choose to forgive as Christ forgives and choose to leave the past in the past, they choose to forgive before forgiveness is needed. In other words, they take the initiative to forgive. This is critical because conflict is going to happen. People are going to let you down and sin against you. You'll be hurt and disappointed. This issue of forgiveness will not go away. It's not a matter of if but when the call to forgive will surface. Because forgiveness is a given in relationships, authentic forgivers choose today to forgive tomorrow.

During His last days on earth, Christ demonstrated His decision to forgive before it was needed. John 13:1 says, "Jesus knew that the time had come for him to leave this world and go to the Father. Having loved his own who were in the world, he now showed them the full extent of his love." His love wasn't merely verbal. He washed the disciples' feet as a physical demonstration. He humbled Himself before those He loved. One by one, He washed the feet of His disciples, including Judas who would betray Him, Peter who would deny Him, and Thomas who would doubt whether He had indeed risen. He also washed the feet of His friends who would fall asleep in the garden when He asked them to keep watch. Jesus knew these things would happen. Yet, in washing their feet, Jesus offered forgiveness before it was needed. What an awesome display of love and forgiveness. If we learn to love like Christ, humbling ourselves before one another, our marriages will be blessed.

> If we learn to love like Christ,
> humbling ourselves before one another,
> our marriages will be blessed.

Why love like this? Jesus explains, "Now that I, your Lord and Teacher, have washed your feet . . . I have set you an example that you should do as I have done for you. . . . Now that you know these things, you will be blessed if you do them" (John 13:14-15,17).

Friends, we all have a Judas who betrays us, a Peter who denies us, and a Thomas who doubts we have much to offer. We have friends who'll sleep when we need them most. It's not a matter of if but when. For our relationships to grow beyond sin and toward authenticity, we must follow Christ's example and choose to forgive before forgiveness is needed. We must take the initiative to forgive. You see, forgiveness always starts with you and not someone else. Matthew 5:23-25 says, "Therefore, if you are offering your gift at the altar and there remember that your brother has something against you, leave your gift there in front of the altar. First go and be reconciled to your brother; then come and offer your gift. Settle matters quickly." Mark 11:25 says, "And when you stand praying, if you hold anything against anyone, forgive him, so that your Father in heaven may forgive you your sins."

Do you get the point? If your brother has something against you, go and work it out. If you have something against your brother, go work it out and forgive him. Regardless of who did what, forgiveness always starts with you. How our relationships would change if we started taking this call to forgive seriously! Authentic forgivers don't wait for their spouse to initiate the transforming power of forgiveness. They forgive before forgiveness is needed, becoming emotional foot washers in their marriage.

Oh, we know forgiveness can be difficult. Some incredibly painful and evil things happen. But the divine power of God gives us everything we need in order to overcome (see 2 Timothy 3:16-17; 2 Peter 1:3-10). In Christ, you'll find all the courage and strength to forgive as Christ forgives, to leave the past in the past, and to forgive before forgiveness is needed. When this happens, an authentic Christ-centered relationship grows into the wholeness that God intended.

18. Ephesians 4:29-32 and Colossians 3:12-14 list things that create conflict or foster forgiveness. Use them to create two lists below.

Creates Conflict/Get Rid Of	Fosters Forgiveness/Replace with This
ex: unwholesome talk	ex: kindness and compassion

19. In the lists above, circle one thing you can get rid of and one thing you need to replace it with in your relationship.

THE WEEK IN ACTION

20. Write the three things that forgiveness is not.

21. Write the three choices of authentic forgivers.

22. What is God asking you to do to be a more authentic forgiver?

A PERSONAL EXAMPLE

I (Dale) learned the true meaning of forgiveness when fishing with my grandfather. We used cane poles on most of our fishing trips, but on this special day, my grandfather pulled out a shiny new Zebco 33. He told me all I had to do was bait my hook, push down the black button, take it back to two o'clock then throw my arm toward twelve o'clock, and let it fly. I followed his instructions, baiting my hook, taking my arm back, and throwing it forward but the line went nowhere. I stood there, beating the water in front of me, making a muddy mess. I looked at him and said, "Papaw, the rod doesn't work!" With a huge grin, he replied, "You forgot to take your finger off the button!"

Friend, that's forgiveness! It's taking your finger off the pain and wrong and releasing it into the hands of Christ. What's something you've been holding on to? Do you have such a tight grip that it's literally gripped you? Just as I beat the water in front of me making a muddy mess of everything, so it is with your soul. Today can be the first day of freedom for you.

23. Come before your loving heavenly Father and ask Him to forgive you. Then, receive and rest in His forgiveness. Write your prayer below.

Lord Jesus, I come to You to be restored through this prayer of confession. I ask that You . . .

24. Release your wounds, hurts, bitterness, and anger into the hands of Christ. Specifically name the person, event, and circumstance. Ask for God's grace to restore your heart. Ask for complete and total forgiveness for the person that wronged you or the person you wronged. Write your answer below.

If you're not sure how to pray, try following this example: *Lord Jesus, I release [name the person or the circumstance] into Your hands. I forgive them, trusting You with my heart. I ask You to remove all bitterness, anger, and resentment in me. I pray for freedom for my soul as I bind my heart and mind to Yours. Please cover every circumstance with Your grace. Restore the joy of my salvation as I am fully restored in Your grace and mercy. Thank You for the power of complete and total forgiveness. I choose to walk in wholeness and authenticity, fully loved, fully forgiven, and fully free because of your finished work on the Cross of Calvary.*

Higher-Risk Option: As we learned, forgiveness always starts with us. Should you go to someone who needs to be forgiven? Do you need to ask for forgiveness from someone? The Word of God is clear and the choice is yours. Will you simply be obedient, do the right thing, and trust God for the rest? Remember, you're not responsible for other people's actions or responses. You are only responsible for you.

Sometimes, face-to-face forgiveness is not possible. People have passed away, moved away, or can't be contacted. If so, we suggest you write a letter to him or her and offer forgiveness. Pray a prayer of release and blessing over their life, and then destroy the letter.

LET IT GO

Luke 7:40-50—Simon and the Woman

What principles of forgiveness did Christ want us to understand?

For the one who stands in need of forgiveness:

Sin must be _____.

Invite the Holy Spirit's help (John 16:13).

Sin _____.

Call it quick (Matthew 5:25).

It's not about the amount of sin, but the awareness of it.

Desperate for _____.

Are you willing to do WHATEVER it takes (Luke 9:23-25)?

Responds in _____.

There is an outward expression of our inward condition (Luke 6:45).

For the one who needs to forgive:

Sin must be _____.

Invite the Holy Spirit's help (John 16:8).

_____ what you have been _____

(Proverbs 3:27).

The result is _____.

Now turn to appendix A (page 177) and record your resolution.

Chapter Eight

MAKING LOVE

For God so loved the world that he gave his one and only Son, that whoever believes in him shall not perish but have eternal life.

John 3:16

Love. We've heard about it from talk shows. We've seen it on television, in the movies, and through the Internet. Love. We use this word with such carelessness. We "love" so many things: sports, cars, careers, and

> Take a moment to open your prayer to the Lord, asking Him to show you what authentic love really looks like and remove any false or fleshly love that is in conflict with His kind of love.

things. We "love" hobbies, activities, our favorite foods, and relationships. Our fleshly nature is often driven by our feelings and responses when in fact love is so much more than a feeling. Too often, couples operate in the world's definition of love instead of God's.

Too often, couples operate in the world's
definition of love instead of God's.

Agape is the Greek word for Christlike love. It means unconditional love—love that remains constant with no strings attached. It involves choosing to love, even when your spouse may be unloving or unlovable. It puts your spouse's interest ahead of your own. Many marriages have been damaged by the selfish "it's all about me" attitude. When husbands and wives focus on themselves and their individual needs, manipulation of the other is usually the result.

Scripture clearly calls all believers to ministry, not manipulation. As Christians, we share the love of God with others in our world, but within the walls of our own homes, we're sometimes extremely self-centered and demanding of love. We don't view our marriages as ministry opportunities and instead focus on our own selfish wants. Seeking wholeness apart from God, we manipulate one another in alarming ways to meet our need for love.

Christlike agape love is the most fulfilling, beautiful part of any marriage relationship. This kind of love involves commitment, determination, and dedication. It's a choice to love. God commands us to love with clear instructions on how and why we should love. In 1 Corinthians 13, God gives us a clear, concise, and detailed description of agape love as the benchmark of the love husbands and wives can share with one another. Consider these five verses:

> *Love is patient, love is kind and is not jealous; love does not brag and is not arrogant, does not act unbecomingly; it does not seek its own, is not provoked, does not take into account a wrong suffered, does not rejoice in unrighteousness, but rejoices with the truth; bears all things, believes all things, hopes all things, endures all things. Love never fails. (1 Corinthians 13:4-8, NASB)*

Have you ever tried to fight with somebody who demonstrates this kind of love to you? You just can't do it. You can try to be mean or harsh or even serious, but when they're showing selfless agape love, you can't fight with them. If you are allowing the 1 Corinthians 13 traits of love to be manifested in your life, it's extremely unlikely that you'll experience unresolved conflict. To have a truly fulfilling marriage, we have to learn to exercise agape love with one another. If agape love is your motivation in all you say or do, then love will never fail, because God's Word promises us just that.

As you consciously make the choice to love, while applying personal responsibility when your actions do not demonstrate love, you'll be able to develop authentic agape love in your life toward others. Truly authentic love is characterized by these four qualities found in God's Word: making love a priority (see Mark 12:30-31), committing to each other (see James 1:12), following through with action (see Romans 5:8), and serving each other (see Philippians 2:5-7).

Keep in mind the deep-rooted needs of intimacy and importance, combined with a backdrop of experience that comes from our family of origin. All these dynamics plus our personal propensity for selfishness and the fact that no one ever explained any of this to us in the first place—much less taught us how to be husbands and wives—lead us many times to act on our most selfish, primitive instincts.

The good news is this: Today you can make a conscious decision to become a minister of love in your marriage, just as Jena and I strive daily to do. Our road of reconciliation has been paved with the conscious decision and commitment to apply the calling of ministry in our marriage. This isn't easy. We've been trained to be manipulators from an early age.

When our daughter Jorja was eighteen months old, she loved strawberry milk. It was a nightly ritual at our house for her to have a glass sometime before bed. One particular evening, Jorja asked for her milk but we didn't have any. As we explained to her that we wouldn't be able to fix her a glass, she looked directly at me (Dale) and began to wink, smile, and show physical affection. Our son Cole looked at Jena and said, "Watch this, Dad's gonna go get her some milk." Sure enough, at ten thirty that night, I drove to the grocery store and bought the milk and strawberry syrup so Jorja could have her way. She was on a

156 ■ LET'S GET REAL

fast track to becoming a master manipulator of her daddy.

Selfishness and a need for personal satisfaction are happening in marriages constantly. Manipulation occurs when a husband and wife act like children in big people's bodies. We must learn to give the unconditional agape ministry of love away to others.

We can't give away what we don't possess. Therefore, we must regularly receive love from the "Lover of our own souls," Jesus Christ, to ever truly understand love in its deepest and fullest form.

....

We can't give away what we don't possess.

....

1. How might the world describe love today?

2. Go back to 1 Corinthians 13:4-8. For each phrase describing love, write its antonym, or opposite.

3. Take an honest look and evaluate where you line up. Mark it on the scale below.

|---|

Worldly Love   Christlike Love

As you study the four characteristics of God's agape love, we pray that you will see areas in your lives that need to change. We pray you'll go from a selfish perspective to a ministry perspective of love. After all,

Christ clearly says that we must decrease so that He can increase. If we want to save our lives, we must lose them. And when we are weak, He is strong. Through the guidance of the Holy Spirit, may manipulation and selfishness be revealed and crucified in our relationships so that His love will permeate our homes for His glory and our joy.

MAKE LOVE A PRIORITY

In Matthew 22 Jesus is at the height of His ministry, and yet the Jewish leaders are questioning His every move. Does your spouse question your every move? Do you question them in the same way? Jesus understands how that feels and He responded with one thing: love. One of the rulers asked Him this: "Out of all the commandments given, which is the most important?" That word, *important,* is the Greek word *protos*, which is where we get our word priority. So when Jesus was asked what should be our priority in life, He answered, "Love."

> Ask the Lord to give you ears to hear, a heart to receive, and the willingness to obey what you learn, in the name of Jesus.

Love was the motivation for everything Jesus did and said. Can that be said of you?

Christ made love the priority of His life. Love was the motivation for everything Jesus did and said. Can that be said of you? We're often motivated by a desire to win, to be right, to be heard, and to get our own way when conflict comes. Jesus Christ made love the center of all that He was. It was priority for Him. Would your spouse say your priority in life is loving God and loving him or her? Or would they say children, careers, or life has taken priority over love for them? It doesn't have to.

We know a couple who are fellow sojourners in the Lord. They challenge us, inspire us, pray for us, and hold us accountable. When we first remarried, our challenge from them was to create a priority time to love each other through the gift of undivided attention. They challenged us to make time for each other every day to reconnect after our time apart. We thought we had that priority time at night after the children went to bed while we watched Andy Griffith together. The reality was that we weren't connecting at all; we were just sitting in the same room watching television. We needed uninterrupted talk time. Our friends also reminded us of this: If God wants us to teach our children what marriage looks like but we take the time to reconnect after the children are asleep, what kind of view are we giving our children of what a healthy, loving marriage looks like? Our children aren't seeing it if they're already in bed asleep! My (Jena) first thought was that I would be missing out on time spent with my children, but the Lord quickly reminded me that time spent making my marriage a priority before them had long-term effects on their future marriages. If they saw us making our marriage a priority, they would make their marriages a priority one day.

So now, as soon as Dale comes home from work, we tell our children, "It's time for Mom and Dad to have some time together. Please don't interrupt us unless there is a major crisis. Otherwise, we'll let you know when we're finished." Then, we sit together in our den and discuss our day with one another. We talk about what happened, how it made us feel, and what we need from each other for the rest of the evening. This practice not only helps us reconnect for the rest of the evening, it shows we're more important to each other than anything else. It also greatly benefits the pressing demands that we encounter the rest of the evening.

Here's what a typical stressful day looked like in our home. I (Jena) would be cooking. I would also be trying to get Jorja to take her bath, answer questions from Cole about a project, and answer the phone. This is when Dale would walk in. Though I asked how Dale's day was, I had a few other things going on. Somewhere in that confusion, Dale would retreat to the recliner because he had no desire to compete for my attention. He'd had a terrible day and now the house was crazy too. So he escaped to the chair. I would get mad at him for not helping me. After all, I had worked just as hard and my day wasn't over until the children were in bed, asleep. So I'd walk upstairs with a basket of laundry and drop it at his feet. That made him mad. After all, he'd worked all day long to provide for his family. The least we could do was show him a little appreciation. By the end of the evening, I was furious and not speaking to Dale, and Dale was infuriated for having to fold sheets. He gave me the silent treatment.

Does this describe your house? This conflict wouldn't have occurred if love had been a priority in our home. If I'd stopped what I was doing and given Dale my undivided attention, I'd have heard about his terrible day, my struggles could have been voiced, and we would understand how the other was feeling. Then we could have been encouragers for the rest of the evening. I (Jena) might have sympathized with Dale's stressful day and actually *wanted* him to head to the recliner and relax, ministering love to my husband. And the same goes if the tables were turned and I'd had a bad day. Had we taken the time to make our marriage a priority, Dale would have known my plight and been able to minister to me. You see, making your love relationship a priority can make all the difference in the world as you reconnect and then minister to one another. As a result, agape love overflows in your home and your children receive an accurate representation of what a God-honoring marriage looks like.

Making your love relationship a priority can make all the difference in the world as you reconnect and then minister to one another.

4. Look at Matthew 22:34-40 and record the three ways we are to love.

5. Why do you think Jesus made these three distinctions?

6. How might they look if you were to put them into practice in your marriage?

May we all determine with everything within us to make loving God and our spouses the priorities of our lives—not just expressed in words, but by the way we live.

COMMIT TO EACH OTHER

> Lord, we thank You already for what You are showing us about Your love. We want Your love to overtake our fleshly, insufficient love, so continue to reveal Yourself and Your love to me as I sit before You. In Jesus' name I ask, Amen.

God also showed His agape love for us by His commitment. We shudder when we think of our society's view of commitment. In today's society, many people refuse to commit for fear they'll have to do something that they don't want to or will miss out on something far better. So their lives are characterized by an endless supply of maybes. They're only as committed as it benefits them. If it's about helping another, but there's nothing in it for them, you can forget it.

We leased a car years ago and quickly found it's easier to get out of a marriage than an automobile lease. Unbelievable amounts of paperwork and loopholes and extra fine-print expenses kept coming up. Yet to file for divorce can be simply signing a few documents, paying a lawyer, and it's done. A completed transaction of terminating a covenant made before the Creator of the universe is easier than terminating a man-made agreement on paper. Something is severely wrong with this picture.

In today's society, many people refuse to commit for fear they'll have to do something that they don't want to or will miss out on something far better.

Today people make empty promises, don't follow through, and then wonder why others don't trust them anymore. It's because their words have been cheapened with unkept commitments. And the Enemy is rejoicing as more relationships are falling apart with every passing day.

When I (Jena) was a child, I remember picking one activity that I would participate in for the year. You can bet if I made a commitment, my parents would see to it that I remained a faithful part of the team or class until the very last day. Why? Because they taught me the value of commitment. They told me that my word was my honor, and if I committed to do something, I was going to do it even if it killed me. That's not the current attitude of our culture. As a matter of fact, we frequently hear people say this about our leaders: They say one thing and then do another; while they talk a good game, they never follow through. As Paul said in Romans, "God forbid!"

For some, commitment only has to be adhered to as long as it makes them feel good. As soon as the feelings go, commitment goes right along with it. If they feel love, they conclude it must be love and they remain in the relationship. But if they don't feel love, then they conclude there must not be love and get out of the relationship and begin searching for someone else who makes them feel love. Hear this one truth: While feelings are often important indicators of something much deeper, that's all that they're good for. They shouldn't determine our behavior unless we first evaluate the whys behind them. They can lead us away from the truth. Our feelings can swing us in all directions. We must be careful about allowing our feelings to determine our behavior and our responses. Properly processing our feelings and walking in truth are critical to marriage.

> ### If we operated solely on our feelings, we'd have a mess on our hands.

If we operated solely on our feelings, we'd have a mess on our hands. If parents only fed their children when they felt like it, there'd be a lot more starving kids in this world. If people only went to work when they felt like it, they wouldn't maintain their jobs for very long. And because people stay committed to their marriages only as long as the feelings are there, the divorce rate is soaring.

The world we live in tells us our feelings lead to action, so when the feelings are gone, stop the actions. God's love explains the opposite. We're commanded to act like we love each other whether we feel like it or not. When we do this consistently, the good feelings follow. The commitment to obeying and trusting God through faith comes first.

The best definition we've heard for faith is by James McDonald, who said, "Faith is believing the Word of God and acting upon it no matter how I feel, because God promises a good result."[1] Now, notice that it doesn't say "the result I want" but rather the result God sees best for me. What if we would simply love our spouse with agape love, not because they deserve it or because we feel like it but simply because God commands it? What if we chose to love them, not because they're worthy but because He is worthy?

....

> "Faith is believing the Word of God and acting upon it no matter how I feel, because God promises a good result."
> —James McDonald

....

What would it have been like if Christ had come to this earth, ministered just as He did, but went to God and said, "Father, these people are a bunch of ingrates. I try and show them Your ways and they don't listen. They don't deserve Your love. Therefore, I have decided not to pay the penalty for their sin." Fortunately, that's not what our Savior did. Our Savior looked mockery in the face and bore the sin of the world. He remained faithful and committed to the end. We're to do nothing less. Living out agape love means you love your spouse by committing yourself and your love to them forever, even during times when the feelings have faded.

7. Which phrase best describes what Jesus was saying in Matthew 15:8? Circle your answer.

- You talk too much!
- You talk a good game, but your heart isn't committed to me!
- You say the right things, but your life doesn't reflect what you say!
- You say you are committed to me, but the truth is, you're not!
- All of the above.

8. Read Ecclesiastes 5:4-5 and record what you believe Solomon was conveying.

9. Match the Scriptures below to their corresponding paraphrase.

Hebrews 12:2	I know God and do what He says.
Matthew 26:39	Not My will but Yours be done.
John 8:55	So for the joy set before Me, I endure the cross.

10. Now, combine those phrases in one sentence that reflects what God requires of us when it comes to loving another.

Maybe you wrote something like this: "Because God has commanded me to love Him and love others, I will choose to love even though it may go against everything I feel like doing, for the joy it will bring to the Lord and to me." Whatever you wrote, know this: When we honor our commitment in marriage before our Father, as Jesus honored His commitment before His Father, He will greatly bless and honor it.

Some of you are divorced and single. Perhaps you need to pray about returning to your spouse and seeking God's help in working through your relationship. Some of you have divorced and are now remarried to someone else. Make your commitment to this marriage for a lifetime.

The most loving thing you can do is to restate your commitment to your spouse. Tell him/her that divorce is not an option and will no longer be used as a threat when conflict occurs. Make your commitment one that is kept and unwavering to the glory and honor of the One who laid before us the perfect example to follow.

FOLLOW THROUGH WITH ACTION

Agape love is proven true in the life of a believer when it is backed by action. "But God demonstrates his love for us in this: While we were still sinners, Christ died for us" (Romans 5:8). Love must also be demonstrated by action in our marriages, not just communicated with our mouths. We all need more than just lip service in our relationships. Have you ever made a comment to your spouse like this: "I shouldn't have to prove myself to

> Make John 15:17 your prayer and ask the Lord to help you fulfill it.

you"? Jesus Christ spent much of His life proving the full extent of His love. He proved His love for us all the way to a cruel, rugged cross. We, too, must spend our lives proving our love for our Savior as well as our love for our spouses through obedience.

We say it like this: When we got married, there was a "trust-o-meter" placed in our relationship. Since then, everything I have done, am currently doing, or will do in the future directly impacts the trust in our relationship. Our actions either demonstrate a love that builds trust or a lack of love that tears it down.

Many of you may have attempted to demonstrate love, but found that it wasn't received. Maybe your spouse continues to say that your actions don't say "I love you" to them. This can be really frustrating if you're trying hard to demonstrate love as best you know how. Author and speaker Gary Chapman has written an incredible book called *The 5 Love Languages*.[2] This book is a must-read for anyone who wants to love their spouse, children, family, and friends in the ways they can best receive and understand. Dr. Chapman shares that there are five tangible ways that people give and receive love. If you're giving love to another person who doesn't recognize love in the way you're giving it, then it's as if you're speaking another language to them.

When Dale and I began to recognize our love languages as well as our children's love languages, we stopped spinning our wheels. We were actually loving each other in ways the other person could understand, and it revitalized our relationships. There was such a newfound energy and excitement in our marriage as we began to demonstrate love to one another in ways the other understood and recognized as love. It was just as incredible to see our children respond because they understood in new ways the depths of their parents' love.

When our daughter Jorja was beginning school, she had a real struggle with separation. She made awful scenes in the school car line as she cried and begged not to have to go to school because she wanted to stay at home. I (Jena) would cry all the way home, begging God to take care of Jorja. Dale offered to take Jorja to school to save me the tears, but he called after the first day crying too. At one point, we considered paying someone to take our daughter to school. With a broken heart, I asked God to help our family survive this struggle and give us discernment about what to do. In His still, small voice, the Spirit of God whispered, "Spend time with Jorja." Well I was a bit miffed at that statement. After all, I stayed home with the children and they were with me a lot of the time. But as I pondered this, I realized that though Jorja was with me, she rarely got my complete attention. Jorja's way of receiving love was through spending quality time together.

When Jorja came home from school the next afternoon, she and I grabbed a quick snack, went out to the trampoline, and worked on spelling together. It only took about twenty minutes, but the next day there were no more tears. The next evening, I got under the covers with Jorja at bedtime and read her a book with the flashlight. The next morning there were no tears. Jorja was no longer struggling with the anxieties of separation because she was experiencing love in a way she could receive it.

11. Where do you think your marriage falls on the scale of your marriage trust-o-meter?

No Trust   Unwavering Trust

12. How much would you say you're demonstrating love to your spouse?

No Demonstration   Much Demonstration

13. Describe the ways you like love demonstrated to you.

14. How would you describe the ways your spouse prefers love demonstrated?

15. Read 1 John 3:16-18 and write verse 18 here.

We must learn to be demonstrators of our love for one another throughout our marriage. When couples first fall in love, they constantly prove their love with all sorts of special gifts, words, and time. As the years go by, the gifts, words, and deeds wane. We must continue to show love to our spouses after marriage. When we demonstrate love to one another regularly, we'll bear healthy, fulfilling fruit in our marriages.

SERVE EACH OTHER

As we come to the end of our study together, we can't stress enough the importance that servanthood plays in the marriage relationship. It is a beautiful characteristic of agape love that many miss due to this self-absorbed world in which we live. Instead of serving others, many of us are consumed with being served. Yet God shows us a better way.

> Instead of serving others, many of us
> are consumed with being served.
> Yet God shows us a better way.

The Greek word for servant is *doulos*. It's a word that implies "someone who gives his or herself up to another's will, a slave, to be devoted to another as you disregard your own interest."[3] Exodus 21:2-6 provides a clear parallel between servant and master:

> *If you buy a Hebrew servant, he is to serve you for six years. But in the seventh year, he shall go free, without paying anything. If he comes alone, he is to go free alone; but if he has a wife when he comes, she is to go with him. If his master gives him a wife and she bears him sons or daughters, the woman and her children shall belong to her master, and only the man shall go free. But if the servant declares, "I love my master and my wife and children and do not want to go free," then his master must take him before the judges. He shall take him to the door or the doorpost and pierce his ear with an awl. Then he will be his servant for life.*

This Scripture is rich with truths about love, servanthood, and marriage through the life example of a Hebrew servant. After he has served his master for seven years, he is faced with the choice to remain a servant or to go free. As the passage continues to unfold, we see that the master gave the servant his wife, and thus his children, and should the servant choose to go free, the master can retain the wife and children, as they belong to the master and not the servant. What a beautiful, scriptural picture of God's gift to husbands, bestowing upon him the blessing of a wife and children. We need to understand that we do not own our spouses, and as parents we do not own our children. Rather, our mates and our children are gifts from God, entrusted to us for the nurture and care they deserve, just as God Himself has nurtured and cared for us. Couples have a great responsibility to honor one another as the true gift and blessing they are from God.

The turning point of this passage occurs in verse 5: "But if the servant declares, 'I love my master and my wife and children and do not want to go free.'" Wow! This slave can go free, but because of love he remains a slave. Because of the love he has for his master, his wife, and his children, he is willing to experience the pain of being marked as a slave forever. The custom was to take the slave to the doorpost and pierce his ear with an awl so everyone who looked upon him would know that he was a *doulos*, or servant, for his master. Why is this so important for marriages today? Because when a couple is sold out to Christ and their love is centered upon servanthood toward one another, their marriage will have a "marked" difference. Their marriage will be different because Christ has made a difference.

Servanthood in marriage—when a husband and wife put each other before themselves—marks them as children of God. God desires that others notice a difference in how you live your life, how you treat your spouse, and how you show love one to another. Servanthood is a visible characteristic of love when Christ is the catalyst.

Though you may think that you have a choice to leave your marriage at any time, if you deeply love the Lord, you will choose not to leave the marriage but to remain and serve your spouse, not because they deserve it, but because He deserves it. You serve your spouse because of your love for your Master, and He commands you to serve.

It is not dependent upon your spouse's worthiness but upon Christ's worthiness. He is worthy of all the love, devotion, and servanthood I have within me.

....

God desires that others notice a difference
in how you live your life, how you treat
your spouse, and how you show
love one to another.

....

This is precisely what Christ demonstrated as He loved us all the way to the cross of Calvary. Philippians 2:1-7 provides us with the depth of Christ's love and His servant heart:

> *If you have any encouragement from being united with Christ, if any comfort from his love, if any fellowship with the Spirit, if any tenderness and compassion, then make my joy complete by being like-minded, having the same love, being one in spirit and purpose. Do nothing out of selfish ambition or vain conceit, but in humility consider others better than yourselves. Each of you should look not only to your own interests, but also to the interests of others.*
>
> *Your attitude should be the same as that of Christ Jesus: Who, being in very nature God, did not consider equality with God something to be grasped, but made himself nothing, taking the very nature of a servant, being made in human likeness.*

Christ is the epitome of a servant. This passage beckons us all to join Him in His call to love one another with such depth that we would lose ourselves completely for another. We're challenged to do nothing out of selfish ambition or personal gain, but in humility, recognizing that we're in desperate need for God's help to love and serve as we ought.

Our attitude and our minds should align with Christ as we see His character outlined before us. He submitted and aligned His will to His heavenly Father, not desiring His equality with God to be more important. But rather He emptied Himself of everything, giving up the very honorable position in the perfect place of heaven and taking on the position of a servant, a *doulos* of His heavenly Father.

Unlike the servant of Exodus 21, Christ didn't get His ear pierced. He was pierced for our transgressions by the nails of a cruel cross. His servant's heart carried Him all the way to Calvary. More than 2,000 years ago, the world was shown what it really means to be a servant.

And being found in appearance as a man, he humbled himself and became obedient to death—even death on a cross! Therefore God exalted him to the highest place and gave him the name that is above every name, that at the name of Jesus every knee should bow, in heaven and on earth and under the earth, and every tongue confess that Jesus Christ is Lord, to the glory of God the Father. (Philippians 2:8-11)

Will you begin to demonstrate the four characteristics of authentic love, perfectly exemplified by our Lord and Savior, Jesus Christ? The beauty of choice is that you get to make it. You can continue to operate in fleshly ways in your marriage or you can choose to try God's ways of love.

16. Read Matthew 20:26-28 and answer these questions.

  a. If you want to become great in the eyes of the Lord, what must you become?

b. Why did Jesus come?

c. What did it require?

17. Colossians 3:22-24 describes the attitude of a slave. How might that describe your attitude as you serve your spouse?

For many of us, the task of serving seems daunting and impossible. Some have never served and this will be a new challenge. Some feel as though all they do is serve, and they are exhausted. Still others are somewhere in between. Be confident of this, God sees you and knows your heart. He will provide you with all you need as you seek to love Him by serving your spouse and others. God has one requirement for His grace: humility. Our attitude must be the same as Christ Jesus as He humbled Himself and became a servant.

A breath of new life came into our marriage when we committed ourselves to receive God's love and then give that love away. We committed to make one another a priority. We committed to love regardless of fickle feelings. We committed to put love into action. And we committed to become servants unto God by serving each other. Authentic agape love requires nothing less than priority, commitment, action, and servanthood. When we do this, God allows our marriages to sing with the psalmist:

I waited patiently for the LORD;
   he turned to me and heard my cry.
He lifted me out of the slimy pit,
   out of the mud and mire;
he set my feet on a rock
   and gave me a firm place to stand.
He put a new song in my mouth,
   a hymn of praise to our God.
Many will see and fear
   and put their trust in the LORD. (Psalm 40:1-3)

THE WEEK IN ACTION

18. What are some practical ways you can demonstrate God-like love by making your marriage a priority?

19. What's one step you can take to express your commitment to your spouse?

20. Name one thing you can do to demonstrate your love for your spouse in a way he or she will understand and receive as genuine love.

21. How can you serve your spouse in a way that will really minister the love of Christ?

Higher-Risk Option: If you feel that your marriage is safe enough to go a little deeper, you may want to ask your spouse how you're doing in the four areas of agape love. You may want to confess the areas you know you have not asked the Lord to develop and work out in your life. You may even want to take each area and together discuss some practical things you can begin to implement in your relationship to build a deeper and stronger love, representing Christ's love in your marriage and home.

MAKING LOVE

John 3:16

"For God so loved the world that he gave his only begotten Son, that whosoever believeth in him should not perish but have everlasting life" (John 3:16).

1. The _____ of Love

"**S**o loved" means "loved in such a way."

It's _____ (1 John 4:16).

The world's love says _____.

God's love says _____.

2. The _____ of Love

"**T**he world was in trouble" (Proverbs 17:17).

It's _____ (Luke 6:32-38; 1 John 3:16).

The world's love says _____.

God's love says _____.

3. The _____ of Love

"**G**ave" means "delivered, offered, ministered."

What? His Son.

Why? To keep on giving.

It's _____ (John 10:10).

"Eternal" means "perpetually"; "life"_____ means

"vitality, animation, excitement."

Those who gave when dating and then quit when married suck

the life out of their marriage.

It's _____ (John 10:10).

The world's love says _____.

God's love says _____.

You cannot _____ what you do not

_____ (1 John 3:8; Hebrews 4:2; Matthew

7:24; Ephesians 5:1; 3:16-18; 1 Peter 3:7; Philippians 1:27).

**Now turn to appendix A (page 177) and record your
resolution.**

MY MARRIAGE RESOLUTIONS

Because my marriage matters, I resolve to:

1. _____

_____

2. _____

_____

3. _____

_____

4. _____

_____

5. _____

_____

6. _____

_____

7. _____

_____

_____

Signature

HOW TO BECOME A CHRISTIAN

This may be the most important section you read in this entire book. Everything else that's written won't compare to what God will do through your life as you surrender to Him. No marriage will ever reach the heights unless both partners are born again. Follow the path below to find salvation and accept Jesus as your Lord. After your decision to follow Christ, you'll never be the same again. May God transform you into the person He desires for you to be as you allow Jesus to become the Savior of your soul and the Lord of your life!

RECOGNIZE THAT GOD LOVES YOU

"For God so loved the world that he gave his one and only Son, that whoever believes in him shall not perish but have eternal life" (John 3:16).

RECOGNIZE THAT YOU HAVE SINNED

"For all have sinned and fall short of the glory of God" (Romans 3:23).

RECOGNIZE THAT SIN'S DEBT MUST BE PAID

"For the wages of sin is death, but the gift of God is eternal life in Christ Jesus our Lord" (Romans 6:23).

RECOGNIZE THAT CHRIST PAID FOR YOUR SINS

"But God demonstrates his own love for us in this: While we were still sinners, Christ died for us" (Romans 5:8).

PRAY AND RECEIVE CHRIST TODAY

"Everyone who calls on the name of the Lord will be saved" (Romans 10:13).

"For he says, 'In the time of my favor I heard you, and in the day of salvation I helped you.' I tell you, now is the time of God's favor, now is the day of salvation" (2 Corinthians 6:2).

Today, you can receive Christ as your Lord and Savior. As you agree with the Scriptures above, simply pray this prayer in your heart:

Dear Jesus, I ask You to forgive me of my sins and come into my heart and life right now. I accept the payment of my sins by the shed blood of Christ. I accept You, Jesus, as my Lord and Savior. Please reveal Yourself to me and become real in my life from this moment forward. Thank You for saving me and giving me eternal life. I love You and commit my life to You. Amen.

WHAT TO DO NOW?

We encourage you to respond to your decision in the following ways:

1. Tell someone. Tell a close friend, your spouse, even tell us. We would love to hear from you.
2. Find a church home that will baptize you and nurture you in your new walk with the Lord.
3. Commit to grow daily in your new Christian life by reading the Bible, praying, and having fellowship with other believers.

NOTES

Chapter Two: Safe Mates
1. *Merriam-Webster's Collegiate Dictionary,* 11th ed., s.v. "available."
2. John Eldredge, *Wild at Heart* DVD series, "A Band of Brothers" (Nashville: Thomas Nelson, 2001).
3. Dr. Kevin Leman, *Sheet Music* (Carol Stream, IL: Tyndale, 2003), 101.

Chapter Three: Empty Hearts, Empty Homes
1. James Strong, *Strong's Exhaustive Concordance of the Bible* (Peabody, MA: Hendrickson Publishers, 2007).
2. Strong.

Chapter Six: Own Your Stuff
1. James MacDonald, *Gripped by the Greatness of God* (Chicago: Moody, 2005), 22.

Chapter Seven: Let It Go
1. James Strong, *Strong's Exhaustive Concordance of the Bible* (Peabody, MA: Hendrickson Publishers, 2007).
2. Strong.

Chapter Eight: Making Love
1. James McDonald, Walk in the Word Radio Broadcast, Step Up series.
2. Gary Chapman, *The 5 Love Languages* (Chicago: Northfield Publishing, 2010).
3. James Strong, *Strong's Exhaustive Concordance of the Bible* (Peabody, MA: Hendrickson Publishers, 2007).

ABOUT THE AUTHORS

Dale and Jena Forehand know firsthand God's power to transform a marriage that, by all appearances, is irreparably broken. In July 1996, after their eight-year marriage had begun to badly unravel, Dale came home and asked his wife to leave. A bitter custody battle ensued, and the couple was granted joint custody in a September 1997 divorce decree. "We walked away feeling all hope was gone," Dale said. "Yet the very presence of God was still working, even through this experience, to draw us closer to Him." The joint custody arrangement would prove providential in their reconciliation. The Forehands remarried on December 21, 1997, the same day their son prayed to receive Christ.

In 1999, Dale and Jena founded Stained Glass Ministries to communicate to other couples the principles of a healthy marriage they wished they had known the first time around. Their ministry has grown, and today the Forehands are sought-after speakers at marriage and family conferences, men's and women's conferences, and retreats around the country. They have written numerous articles on marriage and family topics, been featured on the *700 Club*, and authored *Stained Glass Marriage: Hope for Shattered Homes* (April 2003), which is now retitled and rereleased as *Let's Get Real: Our Journey to Authenticity and Wholeness*. "It's a story about the death, burial, and resurrection of our marriage. But this story is not about us. It is about hope," write the

Forehands in the book's introduction.

Dale graduated from the University of Alabama, where he received a degree in business administration and management. Answering the call to ministry, Dale, now an ordained minister, is a powerful speaker for the cause of Christ, committed to sharing the hope that is found only in an intimate and authentic relationship with Jesus.

Jena graduated cum laude from Samford University with a BA in business administration and marketing and a minor in vocal performance. She is a dynamic speaker called by God to proclaim the love, power, and freedom that come by walking daily with Christ. Out of her own journey toward authenticity, Jena has written and released a forty-day Bible study for women called *Authentic Woman: In Search of the Genuine Article.*

In addition to their conference and speaking ministry, Dale and Jena have an Internet radio program called "Keepin' It Real with Dale and Jena." They have also recorded a DVD series for couples titled *Let's Get Real: Bringing Authenticity and Wholeness to Your Marriage* (NavPress). The Forehands live near Birmingham, Alabama. They have a son, Cole, who attends Samford University, and they home-school their daughter, Jorja. For more information on their ministry, visit them at www.daleandjena.com.

Enhance your study with the DVD!

Let's Get Real DVD with Leader's Guide
Dale and Jena Forehand

This eight-session DVD equips couples to understand their needs and discover how shame, fear, and anger can eat away at a relationship. Use these DVD sessions to accompany the book and learn practical, biblical ways to keep your marriage safe from busyness and to stay emotionally connected.

978-1-61521-721-2

DVD

Bringing Authenticity and Wholeness to Your Marriage

LET'S GET REAL
DALE and JENA FOREHAND